What Leaders Are Saying about
The ABC'S of Financial Success

"Barry Cameron fulfills his twin callings of prophet [preacher] and pastor in his new book entitled, *The ABC's of Financial Success.* He knows how to afflict the comfortable and comfort the afflicted on this topic. And do we ever need it! A few of us need someone to get in our face and confront our selfishness and materialism. Others of us need someone to give us hope and a strategy for recovery. This book has both components. And, of course, good Bible teaching on this subject is especially enlightening and energizing.

"There is so much from both secular society and even the Christian community on this topic that is blatantly self-serving. It is refreshing to finally read something that is thoroughly biblical, practical, and helpful. What Larry Burkett provides from the perspective of a Christian financial planner, Barry Cameron contributes from the vantage point of a megachurch pastor. The theology is solid. The tone is urgent. The appeal is popular. The language is contemporary. The illustrations are fresh. The book is not just readable, it is compelling. Don't pick it up if you have things to do. You will be quickly hooked by its sermonic impact. You won't want to put it down. This book should be required reading for any Christian who wants to practice responsible stewardship of our life and living."

Dr. Ken Idleman, President
Ozark Christian College, Joplin, Missouri

"Barry L. Cameron is respected as an extraordinary church builder and preacher. This book is a testimony to his giftedness as a writer. Barry is a cowboy that has been on the ranch. He's been there and done that. It is written in a language easily understood. He gives a clear picture of his personal struggles and a straightforward explanation of what God says about money and our use of it. I'm certain Barry will be on the hit list of the credit card industry. However, I believe he will be fondly remembered as a no-holds-barred writer who encouraged us to be honest with God and ourselves. If and when this happens, we can joyfully say, 'Free at last, free at last, praise God, I'm free at last.'"

Wayne B. Smith, founding pastor
Southland Christian Church, Lexington, Kentucky

D1367594

"The financial principles spelled out in this book can transform any family and revolutionize any church, providing economic freedom for both. The principles are biblical and workable, and they are presented in a down-to-earth manner that is easily understandable. Copies of this book should be distributed by the churches of America to every one of their families.

"I first met Barry about 15 years ago when he was pastoring a church in Florida. I read an article of his in his church bulletin and recognized immediately that he is a very gifted writer. I have been on his mailing list ever since and have used many of his insightful articles on my radio program.

"Throughout the years I have constantly encouraged Barry to start writing books. Several weeks ago he sent me *The ABC's of Financial Success* to look over and evaluate. I read it while flying to Los Angeles, and my impression is that it is a potential blockbuster. I can imagine hundreds of churches across America purchasing enough copies to give one to each family in their congregations."

Dr. David R. Reagan, Senior Evangelist
Lamb & Lion Ministries of Dallas, Texas

"Every now and then you meet someone or hear or read something that is so radically 'out of the box' that you can't help but stop and notice. You listen, you learn, and you are impacted. This is how I would describe this book and Barry Cameron. Both have much to say, and both will challenge and bless your life."

Cal Jernigan, Senior Pastor
Central Christian Church, Mesa, Arizona

"You can't spend, borrow, gamble, beg, cheat, or steal your way to financial freedom. Debt equates to financial bondage. Barry Cameron's *The ABC's of Financial Success* helps you make wise choices for applying God-given principles to your attitude toward money."

Bob Russell, Senior Pastor
Louisville, Kentucky

"Barry Cameron's *The ABC's of Financial Success* will place you on the road to truly understanding biblically based stewardship. In this day and age where so many are riddled with debt and overwhelmed with the prospects of ever getting out of debt—this book is a must! Barry's abilities to articulate clear and concise principles is a gift from God. Through his insight of God's Word, you will be motivated to put into practice these steps to financial freedom. To miss out on this book is to miss out on all the blessings that God has in store for those who authentically honor the Lord with their wealth."

Dudley C. Rutherford, Pastor
Shepherd of the Hills Church, Porter Ranch, California

"As a cost management consultant to Fortune 500 companies for the past 15 years, I repeatedly find people know what to do but don't know how to do it. I believe the same can be found in most Christian churches. Church members, especially new believers, know the Bible tells us what to do regarding our God-given finances. But until Barry Cameron wrote *The ABC's of Financial Success*, Christians have not had a book that succinctly explains how to implement God's financial principles.

"I never used a dollar of debt to start or sustain my business. What a blessing it has been to never have that burden. By reading *The ABC's of Financial Success*, I pray that thousands of men and women will learn the benefits and blessings of Barry's G.O.O.D. ideas to transform their personal and professional lives."

Tom Pryor, President
ICMS, Inc., Arlington, Texas

"Debt, for many, is a slave master that can rob a person of physical, mental, emotional, and spiritual strength. To be free of financial debt liberates and brings freedom, along with emotional, spiritual, as well as physical and mental health. Barry Cameron has written the freedom manual for guiding churches and individuals to financial health and all the benefits that brings. *The ABC's of Financial Success* is a powerful, practical, and biblically based guide for all Christians who desire to know the liberating power that comes with living a debt-free life."

Dr. Ron Carlson, President
Christian Ministries International, Eden Prairie, Minnesota

"Barry Cameron, in his book, *The ABC's of Financial Success*, defines some profound truths concerning personal responsibility for financial management. These truths are Biblical, practical, and achievable. It is a book I recommend for individuals, families, and churches who look upon all of life as a stewardship relationship with God. My wife and I have practiced many of the principles defined by Barry and have proved to our own satisfaction that they work. Christians are called to be stewards of God's creation. *The ABC's of Financial Success* can be an invaluable guide for those who want to fulfill that calling."

Dr. Marshall J. Leggett, Chancellor
Milligan College, Milligan College, Tennessee

"Barry Cameron has written a book of financial principles that are easy to understand, practical, and doable for the average person and church. It's a book that doesn't give 'pie-in-the-sky,' unworkable ideas or formulas. Rather, it gives us challenges we need to hear in our personal lives and in our churches that can be started today. *The ABC's of Financial Success* is a hard book to put down."

C. Scott Greer, Senior Pastor
Paramount Terrace Christian Church, Amarillo, Texas

"Financial struggles thwart the potential success of most Christians and the churches they serve. The answers leading to freedom and the maturation that follows are spiritual. Barry Cameron addresses them in a straightforward fashion with a track record of achievement that demands he be heard. Every church leader would be well served to read his stuff. Personally and professionally, I have practiced much of what he espouses in this book. It works!

"His approach is forthright! Straight up! Hard hitting! Heart to heart! He will make you angry, because you know he is right and you had the same insight he did but didn't have the courage to set sail with it. This is not a book you read while sitting on the patio sipping iced tea. It produces no 'warm and fuzzies.' It's what you turn to when all the gimmicks and short-cuts to victory have failed, and you finally choose to return to the basics."

Gary York, Senior Pastor
Eastview Christian Church, Bloomington, Illinois

"You hold in your hand a training manual for financial freedom, written by one who has challenged the status quo and conquered the obstacle course of debt. If you believe that God wants to raise up an army of debt-free, lifetime tithers who are free from bondage and who bless the church, then Barry Cameron is the perfect Drill Sergeant. This book is spiritual boot camp for anyone who is tired of using their future to pay for their past, and no church that teaches these principles will fail to bless God and others in remarkable ways."

Larry Winger, CEO
Church Development Fund, Anaheim, California

The ABC's of Financial Success

The ABC's of
Financial Success

BARRY L. CAMERON

College Press ✠ Joplin, Missouri

The ABC's of Financial Success

Published by College Press Publishing, www.collegepress.com

The author is donating all royalties from this book to create a foundation which will provide financial assistance for retired ministers. For additional information regarding this foundation or to make a contribution you may contact the author at (817) 557-2277 or acc@arlingtonchristianchurch.org

Library of Congress Cataloging-in-Publication Data

Cameron, Barry L. (Barry Lee), 1955-
  The A, B, C's of financial success / Barry L. Cameron.
      p.   cm.
  Includes bibliographical references.
  ISBN 0-89900-824-0 (pbk.)
  1. Finance, Personal—Religious aspects—Christianity.
I. Title.
HG179.C3145 2001
332.024—dc21

                                                    2001047689

Dedication

To Janis, Katie, Matt and Kelli,
for sharing the vision and making the sacrifices
so we could be debt free.

To the Arlington Christian Church family,
the most generous church in America.

Acknowledgments

My special thanks to our wonderful church family, the Arlington Christian Church, for putting these principles into practice and seeing the difference they have already begun to make in our lives and in our ministry.

To Mel Dietz, our administrator, who is a genius when it comes to managing and administrating a church.

To Tom Pryor, who has constantly encouraged me to write.

To Shawn Bowman, for originally putting these words into print.

To Vicki Dietz, my administrative assistant, who for fourteen years has made me look much better than I am.

Table of Contents

Foreword

I have read many books over my lifetime, but when it comes to a book with uniqueness and immediate impact, I can't remember one that has made such an impression on me. To put this in perspective, I need to tell you the background of my first glimpse of this book.

As the Chief Operating Officer at Church Development Fund, Inc., I get the opportunity to work with Christian Churches all across the country. As someone who spent most of my professional life in the "for-profit world," the change to the "not-for-profit world" was very dramatic. In fact, I know God put me through many challenges professionally over a twenty-year period to prepare me for the opportunity to work at CDF and assist churches with their financial challenges in creating new facilities and growing the Kingdom.

I was introduced to Arlington Christian Church in Arlington, Texas, located in the Dallas-Fort Worth metroplex, in the fall of 2000. This church, under the leadership of Barry Cameron, has seen rapid growth in its attendance. Nothing abnormal for a church located in a thriving area with new rooftops popping up in every direction, a dynamic Senior Pastor, and a forward-thinking eldership. But there was something unique, something I felt from the first time I met this group of men.

The church was running over 1600 in attendance on Sunday, was bursting at the seams with its current facilities, and had recently purchased a new site consisting of 101 acres of land. My experience would tell me they probably were below the national average of per capita giving each Sunday, growing and reaching many new believers who weren't givers, cash poor, their current facilities were leveraged, stretched each week to meet their expenses because of their rapid growth, and understaffed since they didn't have the financial resources to add much-needed staff.

When I first met the elders, I saw a group of very confident and competent men and I saw a senior pastor who loved his flock and was dedicated to each and every member. After meeting with the elders and touring the facilities, I returned to my hotel room with a feeling of "WOW, this is a church on fire for the Word of God."

The next morning I returned to the church to get into the details of helping them analyze their financial picture and see how they could move forward with their new site. When I sat down with Mel Dietz, Business Administrator, I was amazed by what I was seeing. Arlington Christian Church had a per capita giving of 2.5 times the national average (this with a growing congregation and today that ratio is probably 3.5 times the national average), they had cash of over $750,000, easily met their expenses each week, and were staffed correctly and pursuing new staff. I said to myself, "Lord, help me out here."

As I concluded my meetings and began to prepare to go

back to DFW Airport for my return trip to Southern California, Barry Cameron gave me a tape series he had preached in January 2000 called *The ABC's of Financial Success*. I thanked him, headed for the airport, and proceeded home. On the plane I pulled out the financial statements again, and as I studied them even more, I was impressed at the financial success of ACC.

When I arrived at John Wayne Airport and began my trip home to Mission Viejo, I popped the first tape of *The ABC's of Financial Success* into the cassette player. I was intrigued as I listened to the first tape titled "Attitude." On my way to our office in Anaheim the next morning, I listened to the second tape, "Bondage," and with a 40-minute commute each way every day, I was able to listen to all four tapes within a day and a half. From these sermon tapes, Barry Cameron had challenged his congregation and leadership. The principles had been put to work and accomplished in a very short time frame. God did the following through this sermon series:

1. Challenged each member to get out of bondage (debt).
2. Challenged the leadership of the church to pay off all of the church debt within 18 months.
3. Challenged the leadership to build mission funds and specific scholarship funds over the next 2 years of $500,000.

These challenges in themselves were demanding, aggressive, and bold. But what you need to know is, I had just studied the church's financial statements and they had accomplished the following:

1. The debt was paid off in less than 6 months and their existing facilities were free and clear of any debt!
2. The special funds had reached over $750,000 in less than 10 months!

Why and how did this happen? I am convinced that God blessed this church because they followed *The ABC's of Financial Success*. They studied the Word on how to be better stewards, and their leadership followed these principles in their personal lives and were examples to the flock. God is truly an amazing God, and ACC has been blessed by their *attitude* (A of the ABC's), their understanding of the *bondage* of debt (B of the ABC's), their *choices* (C of the ABC's), and their *decisions* (D of the ABC's) when it comes to putting God first in their financial lives (*encouragement*—E of the ABC's).

I have challenged myself to begin to follow the ABC's. As Chairman of the Elders at Mission Viejo Christian Church, I have challenged our leadership to also follow the ABC's and have encouraged everyone to listen to the tapes. It is our goal at Mission Viejo Christian Church to give our entire congregation the opportunity to read this book.

Whenever we invest something, from a financial perspective, we seek a return on our investment. This book will generate a higher yield than any investment advisor can guarantee. It is a book that will have a very clear message for all those who open its cover. You will find yourself wanting to share this book with a friend. For all of you pastors out there, it is must reading for your leadership and entire congregation. Enjoy!

Douglas J. Crozier
Chief Operating Officer
Church Development Fund, Inc.
April 2, 2001

Introduction

Drive onto the parking lot of the average church in America. You'd be led to believe that Christians have to be among the very best money managers on earth. You'll see Lincoln Continentals, BMWs, a few Corvettes, a number of Dodge Rams and Ford F-Series trucks, some Cadillacs, lots of SUVs, a Jaguar or two, and a few P.T. Cruisers.

However, once you go inside and see what the average offering is for these same churches, you know immediately something is wrong.

For example, our church in Arlington has about 550 parking spaces and we will fill those spaces three different times, with three different sets of vehicles each Sunday. For the sake of illustration, and to be on the conservative side, let's say those 1650 different vehicles are only worth $10,000 each. (I'm quite confident my figures are on the low side.) That comes to a whopping figure of $16.5 million dollars worth of metal, glass, rubber, and leather, pulling onto our church parking lot every Sunday morning.

Let's take it a step further. Let's say those 1650 vehicles represent 825 different homes. And let's say those 825 different homes are only worth $50,000 each. (Again, my figures are intentionally on the low side.) That would come to an incredible figure of $41,250,000.

Let's go another step. Let's say those 825 homes represent an annual income of $40,000. (Again, a conservative estimate for the Dallas/Fort Worth area.) That would mean that the combined annual income of the people who attend our church would be somewhere in the neighborhood of $33 million dollars.

Now follow me. That would mean, on any given Sunday, the people who attend worship at our church could collectively represent a net worth (conservatively, remember) of over $90,750,000.

Our current average weekly offering (which is above average for churches in America our size) is around $65,000 each week. Got a calculator?

Several things are glaringly obvious: *One*, we are not reaching our potential when it comes to financial stewardship. *Two*, we need to do a better job of teaching on money and financial issues. *Three*, our people are probably in some serious debt. And *four*, we are not nearly as good at managing our money and resources as we think we are. This book is about changing all that.

My prayer is that you will consider the purchase of this book one of the best investments you've ever made, and that it will pay dividends for the rest of your life.

Barry L. Cameron, Senior Pastor
Arlington Christian Church

. . . from the G.O.O.D. file

(simple ideas to encourage you to Get Out Of Debt)

Have you ever stopped to think what it would be like to be completely DEBT FREE? A lot of people live their entire lives thinking and believing it would be impossible for them to ever achieve the goal of being debt free. But, what if it weren't? (And it isn't! Being debt free is within reach of *anyone* who *wants* to reach that goal.)

What if it were possible for *you* to be totally and completely DEBT FREE? Think about it! Can you imagine what you could do?

Solomon wrote in Proverbs, "Where there is no vision, the people perish" (29:18, KJV). He also wrote, "As a man thinks in his heart, so is he" (23:7, NKJV). So, if having a vision and having the right thinking is that important, maybe you and I should do some Christ-centered vision casting of our own and start thinking about what we could do if we were totally debt free.

Here are just a few suggestions to help you get started:

1. You would be free to give to God and the church like you always wanted to.
2. You could start doing whatever you want with your money. (Imagine more money than bills!)
3. You would have no outstanding debts except that continuing debt to love one another.
4. You could put money in savings and earn lots of interest for a change instead of paying it.
5. You could help your immediate and extended family.
6. You could finally have that "dream" vacation.
7. You could fix things up around your house or even get a new one.
8. You could get some new furniture or a new vehicle.
9. You could surprise people with secret acts of kindness and generosity.
10. You could do almost anything you can imagine.

Action Plans

Now, here's the point. If we don't *think* we can be debt free, we never will be. But if all we do is think about it and dream about it and don't start DOING SOMETHING about it, it won't happen.

So, take some G.O.O.D. advice: 1) sit down and make out a *wish* list of all the things you'd like to do once you're debt free. Then, 2) make a list of all the things you *need* to do in order to get debt free. Once you've done that, get to work on list #2 (the list of things you need to do). And, each week and each month, as you are able to check something off your "to do" list, you are one step closer to being able to check things off list #1 . . . and seeing your dreams come true!

A Chapter 1
Attitude

"The greatest discovery of my generation is that a human being can alter his life by altering his attitude."
—William James

SECRET SANTA

You don't know his name, nobody does, and that's the way he wants it. But you'll never forget what I'm about to tell you. They call him Secret Santa, and the week before Christmas in 1999 he handed out $85,000 in $100 bills to unsuspecting people on the streets of Kansas City.

The story actually begins in 1971, in Houston, Mississippi, a small county seat town. The man who would become

Secret Santa was then a young salesman. Every week his employer would send him a paycheck and pay rent on a small office and a room at a local motel. But one day the employer went out of business and failed to tell the young man. After losing his motel room for nonpayment, the young man slept in his car for eight nights. He kept waiting for a paycheck that never arrived. Out of gas and money, he turned to a local church for assistance. The person who supervised the fund to help the poor was gone the day he inquired. The next morning he walked into the Dixie Diner, a small brick café around the corner from Walgreen's in Houston, Mississippi. Having not eaten for two days, he ordered a huge breakfast and slowly sipped coffee refills, wondering how he could escape without paying. Finally, he pretended to lose his wallet. The owner, who was also the cook, waiter, and cashier, lifted a countertop door and walked behind the young man's leather-covered stool, reached toward the floor, and acted as if he picked something up. "You must have dropped this," the owner said, handing the young man $20. The young salesman's heart was pounding as he paid, left a tip, raced outside and pushed his car to a gas station before fleeing. As he drove away, he thought about how fortunate he was. Suddenly it occurred to him that no one had dropped that money. The man behind the counter knew he was in trouble and helped him in a way that allowed him to keep his dignity. "If I'm ever in a position to help other people," he told himself, "that's what I'm going to do."

Later that year that young salesman rode a Greyhound bus to Kansas City where he found a sales job and continued living from paycheck to paycheck. Today he is a wealthy Jackson County businessman who regularly hands out $50,000 or more during each of his Christmas campaigns, which he has been doing now for over 20 years. Last year Secret Santa located the Mississippi diner owner, Mr. Ted Horn. He told Mr. Horn he was doing research on Secret Santa and wanted to come down and meet him. When they met, Mr. Horn said he always wanted to meet Secret Santa himself because he remembered the guy and remembered the $20. "It was in my diner where it happened," he said. "I know, Mr. Horn," Secret Santa revealed, "I was that young salesman."

"By the way, what do you reckon that $20 bill is worth today? Do you know how to figure net present value? I had somebody figure that for me." Before Secret Santa could tell Horn the answer, which was about $120, Horn gave a response that fit right into Secret Santa's plans. He said, "Well, to me that $20 bill then was probably like $10,000 to you today." "Funny you should say that," Secret Santa replied as he pulled out an envelope full of $100 bills with a strap of paper around it that said $10,000. "You don't have to do this," Horn said softly. "But I wanted to," Secret Santa replied. "You never know what one little act of kindness will do for somebody. It can change their whole life. You sure changed mine."[1]

You are holding in your hands a life-changing book, *The ABC's of Financial Success*. Next to the Bible it might be the most important book you've ever read because of the principles you're going to learn. In fact, it's very possible you will look back on this book and realize it was one of the greatest things that ever happened to you. I believe, for some people, they'll look back and say, "You know what, that book was worth a million dollars to me." It might as well be you.

So let's get started.

INTEREST NOT SO INTERESTING

The average person doesn't really believe he has a problem when it comes to finances. He really doesn't. As long as he's making monthly payments on time, as long as he has some mad money he can play with each week, as long as he can continue to feed and satisfy those occasional indulgences from time to time, he erroneously believes things are just fine. Unfortunately he's like the alcoholic, the drug addict, the gambler, or the person addicted to pornography who says, "I don't have a problem." But the truth is, the average American has a major problem when it comes to money, Christians included. They are horribly in debt, miserable managers of their money, and gullible beyond belief when it comes to buying things on credit. Can I share a simple principle with you? If you're paying interest on anything, regardless of the great interest rate you may have gotten or the low monthly payment; if you are paying interest on anything, are you ready for this? YOU ARE LOSING MONEY.

In fact, when you see the word "interest," if you visualize two words in huge, gigantic letters as if they were written in the sky, "SOMEBODY ELSE," that will help you better comprehend the principle. Why? Because that's exactly what happens every time you're paying interest. SOMEBODY ELSE is getting rich off YOUR money. Yet so many people say, "Well, you know, we got a great interest rate." Or, "Luckily I got the same low monthly payment on this car that I had on my last one."

Christian financial expert, Larry Burkett, says, "Christians are now paying nearly 10% of our income every year in interest alone. And yet we give only 2% back to God."[2] So here's the picture. The average Christian in America is miserably over his head in debt and walking in rebellion towards God. We definitely have a problem. But you'd better be reasonably bold and considerably courageous if you attempt to suggest to someone he has a problem with his finances. Why? Because we're very touchy when it comes to our stuff. When it comes to my money and my finances, that's a private matter and it's none of your business. Isn't that pretty much the way you feel?

So if someone suggests we have a problem with our finances, we immediately get defensive and go into denial because none of us wants to admit we have a problem.

HARRY TRUMAN VERSUS THE VOLCANO

Do you remember Harry Truman? Not the President. The man who lived on the side of Mount St. Helens in Washington? I'll never forget the guy. He had 23 cats. (Does that help?) Well, back in 1980 he was on Mount St. Helens. TV reporters were interviewing him while the mountain was shaking behind him. Harry's sitting there with his 23 cats and seismologists were saying, "This mountain's gonna blow." Volcanic experts were saying, "This mountain's gonna blow." Harry Truman said, "I don't believe a single one of your experts. I've lived here all my life. I know this old mountain better than anybody else. I'm not going anywhere." And they'd banter back and forth.

I remember his sister on national television (you may remember watching). She pleaded with her brother, "Please, get off this mountain. It's gonna blow." "No, it's not," Harry insisted. "I've lived here all my life. I don't have a problem."

On May 18th, 1980, at 8:31 a.m., the mountain blew. It blew with a force 500 times greater than the power of the bomb that was dropped on Hiroshima. Twenty-five hundred feet blew off the top of the mountain. It blackened the sky from Seattle to New York and as far south as Oklahoma.

No one has ever seen a trace of Harry or his 23 cats since.

DECLARING FINANCIAL INDEPENDENCE

Now I'm praying there are no Harry Trumans reading this book. I'm going to assume you want God's wisdom, God's guidance, and God's provision in your life. I'm going to assume you want to be out of debt and once and for all, as unbeliev-able as this may seem, to be free from the albatross of finan-cial burdens, bills, and bondage.

I'm going to be intensely practical in these few chapters. I'm going to tell you things you won't believe you've read. I'm going to open up my own home, literally, to you. I'm going to tell you how we handle our finances, how we do our budget, and I'm going to walk you through the mistakes we've made.

You're going to be so encouraged by our personal story of finances that you'll say, "Thank you, God, there's hope for all of us." I'm going to share with you the struggles and the suc-cesses from our own church. How we went from being a small church, miserably in debt and struggling just to pay bills, to a church reaching thousands and giving millions each year.

So keep reading.

I'm going to tell you who's behind your financial prob-lems, and when you find out it's not you, you're going to be in shock. It'll get your attention. I'm going to tell you how every one of us can be totally and completely out of debt. It's possi-ble for anyone reading this book. In fact, regardless of how much debt you have today, I agree with Larry Burkett, who says in seven years anybody can be out of debt.[3] Anybody. That includes you, and it includes your church.

Our church is completely out of debt. We've been that way since February 6th, 2000. Our current property and facil-ities are valued at over 8 million dollars and are all paid for. The truth is, we've been a debt-free church since 1995 because that's when we decided to declare our financial independence and never go in debt again.

Our family did the same thing. We declared our financial independence in December of 1999. We decided we were sick of debt and developed a strategy so we could be completely debt free in two years. And guess what? It works!

I was in our church prayer room one Sunday morning, and talk about pressure on the preacher. The head of our Prayer Partner Ministry prayed that God would get the preacher out of debt. He knew I'd already made the commitment. My wife and I made the commitment to be totally out of debt in two years. Someone will say, "You must've had a small amount of debt." No, we had a large amount of debt. But we made a commitment before God, altered our lifestyle, and changed the way we did things. We put our whole family on a budget. I'm on a budget; my wife's on a budget; our kids are on a budget. In fact, the common line heard around our house over the last year or so has been: "Well, that's not in my budget."

We went out to dinner on New Year's Eve and my wife said, "Now, who's paying for this meal? Is it coming out of my budget or your budget?" It came out of mine. (To be honest, it wasn't worth it.) One night we were ordering pizza and I said, "Now, whose budget is going to cover this?" My wife said, "Oh, I'll take that out of mine."

All of us can be out of debt if we really want to be. But we have to want to. I want to help you "want to." That's why I've written this book. I don't want to hurt you, I want to help you. But if we don't begin with step number one, nothing else we talk about will help. We need to begin with *your attitude* toward money.

YOUR ATTITUDE TOWARD MONEY

Look at the words of David in 1 Chronicles 29:10-14. The Bible says,

> David praised the LORD in the presence of the whole assembly, saying
> "Praise be to you, O LORD,
>   God of our father Israel,
>   from everlasting to everlasting.

Yours, O LORD, is the greatness and the power
    and the glory and the majesty and the splendor,
    for everything in heaven and earth is yours.
Yours, O LORD, is the kingdom;
    you are exalted as head over all.
Wealth and honor come from you;
    you are the ruler of all things.
In your hands are strength and power
    to exalt and give strength to all.
Now, our God, we give you thanks,
    and praise your glorious name.

But who am I, and who are my people, that we should be able to give as generously as this? Everything comes from you, and we have given you only what comes from your hand."

David acknowledged the sovereignty of God over everything he had. If you and I are going to have financial success in our personal life, our family, our business, and in our church, then we're going to have to do the same. We're going to have to change our attitude toward money.

LIES THAT SOUND LIKE THE TRUTH

I'm going to share with you several lies that sound like the truth. When you read them you're going to say, "You know, they sound true"—but they're not.

Lie #1: All the church talks about is money.

Remember, don't be misled. It's a lie. The church doesn't talk *enough* about money and how to manage it. Consequently Christians are among some of the worst money managers in the world, even though they ought to be the best.

I have a number of banker friends. They tell me the worst risk for a bank is usually a church. That's why they don't like to extend loans to churches. The reason they don't want to is because churches are notorious for not paying off their loans and often end up going into receivership. No lending institution in its right mind wants to have the public relations nightmare of having to foreclose against a church.

If that weren't bad enough, you know after the church who's the #2 risk to banks? Tragically, it's the pastor of the church. In far too many cases he's one of the worst financial managers there are. I always get nervous when I'm around pastors who want to know if there are discounts for them. (I've never asked for a discount in my life.) I've always said, "You pay me a salary and I'll do like everybody else. I don't need discounts." When somebody offers me a discount, I always say, "No thank you. I'll pay the regular price, whatever it is."

Christians, especially pastors, ought to be leading the world in the management of money, but we don't. Why? I believe Lie #1, all the church talks about is money, trips more people up than we know. Here's how it works: The devil convinces you that all the church talks about is money. So whenever the issue of money comes up, you're already offended. Whether it's a Sunday school class, a cell group, or you're out with Christian friends and the subject of money comes up, if the devil's convinced you that all the church talks about is money, you're already set to be offended.

Why does he do that? SO YOU AND I WON'T LISTEN TO GOD'S TRUTH. If the devil can get you upset or fired up, you won't listen up and you'll miss the truth that can set you free! (Some of you are upset right now. Be honest. Aren't you? You're nervously squirming as you read this. Take three deep breaths and calm down.)

The devil sets us up so we won't listen to what God wants us to know. And as long as we don't know what God wants us to know, we can't possibly do what God wants us to do, and the result? The devil is able to keep us in bondage.

What do we need to do to avoid that? We need to change

our attitude right in the face of the devil. We need to say, "My church needs to talk more about money and help people like me solve our financial problems and get out of debt!"

Lie #2: Money and things can satisfy me.

It sure sounds like the truth, doesn't it? But it's a lie. Money and things can't satisfy you. Money and things can satisfy for a while, but that's it.

Some of you will read this whole chapter and when you get in your car to go to work tomorrow you'll still believe this lie. I could write a hundred chapters on it, preach a hundred sermons on it, and some of you would still walk out the front door of your house tonight or tomorrow morning and say, "Well, I know what he says, but if I had that new car, I'd be pretty happy." "If I had that big house up on the hill overlooking the lake, I'd be pretty happy."

That's my point. We just don't believe it. But you need to know, IT'S A LIE! Every day we're bombarded with advertisements from Madison Avenue and Hollywood about things we need to get or have to have because they'll satisfy us. Oh, really? Ecclesiastes 5:10 says, "Whoever loves money never has money enough; whoever loves wealth is never satisfied with his income. This, too, is meaningless. As goods increase, so do those who consume them. And what benefit are they to the owner except to feast his eyes on them?"

You and I need to change our attitude. Money and things will never satisfy us. Only God can do that. That new car, that new house, that new suit, that new job, that new promotion, it's not going to satisfy you. Only God can do that.

Lie #3: It's my money and I can do whatever I want with it.

When I say this one, especially out loud, it really sounds like the truth. But it's a lie. The truth is, it's all God's money and you and I are simply managers of it. Psalm 24:1 says, "The earth is the LORD'S and everything in it, the world, and all who live in it."

Let me share with you a parable Jesus told. Luke 12:16,

And he told them this parable: "The ground of a certain rich man produced a good crop. He thought to himself, 'What shall I do? I have no place to store my crops.'

"Then he said, 'This is what I'll do. I will tear down my barns and build bigger ones, and there I will store all my grain and my goods. And I'll say to myself, [notice how many times he says, "I, I'll, my, myself,"] "You have plenty of good things laid up for many years. Take life easy; eat, drink and be merry."'

"But God said to him, 'You fool! This very night your life will be demanded from you. Then who will get what you have prepared for yourself?'"

Now don't read into this what the devil wants you to read into it. The devil wants you to hear that when you get a certain amount of things in your life, God's going to yank you home to heaven. That's not what this is talking about. God's not against you having things. What Jesus is saying here is that this guy didn't have a clue. He thought he had all these wonderful possessions and could just sit back and enjoy them for a long time.

The reality is, when we die, all that stuff goes to somebody who didn't work for it anyway. I don't want to frighten you, but all the possessions you have and all the money you've got in the bank, one of these days, it's going to belong to somebody else, and, in most cases, it will belong to somebody who didn't deserve it. You're going to leave it all behind. I'm going to leave it all behind. Job said, "Naked I came into this world, and naked I will go out of this world" (Job 1:21, paraphrase). We're going to leave it all behind. It's not ours. It all belongs to God.

So we need to change our attitude. We need to realize

everything we have is on temporary loan from God, and it's our privilege to be a faithful manager of it for the time we're here on earth. It's just on temporary loan. Those clothes you're wearing, sir, are on loan from God. That nice car you're driving today, ma'am, is on loan from God. That beautiful home you have that God's blessed you with, you guessed it, is on loan from God for a little while. Be a faithful manager of it.

I've shared with you several lies that sound like the truth. Now let me give you some truths that sound like lies. Are you ready?

TRUTHS THAT SOUND LIKE LIES

Truth #1: God is the One Who determines how much money I have.

In Deuteronomy 8:17-18 Moses says, "You may say to yourself, 'My power and the strength of my hands have produced this wealth for me.' But remember the LORD your God, for it is he who gives you the ability to produce wealth, and so confirms his covenant, which he swore to your forefathers, as it is today." In other words what he's saying is, you can go out there and say, "I did this. My hands did this." The truth is, you had nothing to do with it. God's the One who gave you the ability to do it.

In Matthew 6:33 Jesus said, "But seek first God's kingdom and His righteousness, and then all these things will be added to you" (paraphrase). Jesus said, "Don't go after the things. The pagans run after all the stuff. You put God first and God will take care of everything else." Why? Because God is the One Who determines how much money we have; we don't. You and I need to change our attitude. God is the One Who determines my income, not me, not my company, not my hard work, not my brilliance, not my creativity. Therefore, I will put God first.

Truth #2: God has the power to shut down my company, my business, and dry up my source of income without a moment's notice.

Remember the story of Nebuchadnezzar in Daniel 3? He saw what happened to Shadrach, Meshach, and Abednego and said, "Their God has to be THE God. Everybody has to honor their God, and anybody who doesn't will be put to death" (paraphrase). Remember that? In Daniel 4:29 the Bible says, "Twelve months later [one year], as the king was walking on the roof of the royal palace of Babylon, he said, 'Is not this the great Babylon I have built as the royal residence, by my mighty power and for the glory of my majesty?'"

Nebuchadnezzar is walking around admiring his stuff. He's saying, "Wow, look at this. This is all mine. I did all this. Look what's been accomplished through my life and look at this business I've built, and I've got all the bills paid and look at this stuff I've got. Things are going wonderful." And the Bible says,

> The words were still on his lips when a voice came from heaven, "This is what is decreed for you, King Nebuchadnezzar: Your royal authority has been taken from you. You will be driven away from people and will live with the wild animals; you will eat grass like cattle. Seven times [or seven years] will pass by for you until you acknowledge that the Most High is sovereign over the kingdoms of men and gives them to anyone he wishes."
> Immediately what had been said about Nebuchadnezzar was fulfilled. He was driven away from people and ate grass like cattle. His body was drenched with the dew of heaven until his hair grew like the feathers of an eagle and his nails like the claws of a bird.

In the next verse Nebuchadnezzar takes the pen and says, "I'd like to share my testimony. At the end of that time, I, Nebuchadnezzar, raised my eyes toward heaven, and my sanity was restored." I wish I could park there for about a half hour. Get your eyes on God and your sanity will be restored. (There's a sermon there.)

Nebuchadnezzar said,

> Then I praised the Most High; I honored and glorified him who lives forever.
>
>> His dominion is an eternal dominion;
>>> his kingdom endures from generation to generation.
>>
>> All the peoples of the earth
>>> are regarded as nothing.
>>
>> He does as he pleases
>>> with the powers of heaven
>>> and the peoples of the earth.
>>
>> No one can hold back his hand
>>> or say to him: "What have you done?"
>
> At the same time that my sanity was restored, my honor and splendor were returned to me for the glory of my kingdom. My advisers and nobles sought me out, and I was restored to my throne and became even greater than before. Now I, Nebuchadnezzar, praise and exalt and glorify the King of heaven, because everything he does is right and all his ways are just. And those who walk in pride he is able to humble.

God has the power to shut down my company, my business, and yes, even my church and dry up my source of income on a moment's notice. So you and I need to change our attitude. We need to say, "I don't need to worry about the economy or the stock market. Instead I need to focus on living my life in a manner that honors and pleases God." What happens on Monday morning when Wall Street opens is not nearly as important as what happens on Sunday morning as God's people gather together on God's day in God's house to listen to

God's Word. We are acknowledging that God is the One Who can lift us up or shut us down. Any time He wants. We're not in control, God is. He's sovereignly in control of all things and all of us.

Truth #3: Giving to God is the only way out of my financial problems.

Sounds like a lie, doesn't it? Giving to God is the only way out of my financial problems. (I know what you're thinking.) But Jesus said, "Give, and it will be given to you."

I've been in ministry for 29 years, and in all those years I've watched people get into financial difficulty and financial problems, and the first place they cut back is in their giving to God. You can mark it down, sign it, seal it, and take it to the bank, when people get mad at the preacher or get mad at the church, the first thing they do is stop giving to God. You want to say to those people, "It's all right to get mad at me, but don't cut yourself off from the blessings of God."

There will be times when you disagree with your pastor (I know that's hard to believe) or you might get mad at something that happens in the church. But don't stop obeying God just because you're mad at somebody or some thing. You're just going to compound your problems and exacerbate your frustrations.

Someone will say, "Well, preacher, surely you aren't telling me, with the problems I've got and the debt I've got, that I ought to be giving back to God? God wouldn't want me to give, would He?" I've heard well-meaning preachers say, "Oh, no, God understands. God wouldn't want you to give." God doesn't say that. The people who are in financial difficulty are the very people who need to give. Why? I'll let Jesus answer it. "Give, and it will be given to you" (Luke 6:38).

I'm told there's an old shack out in the Arizona desert. Inside this shack is a water well, a pump, a jar of water, and a note. The note says: "If you use this water to prime the pump, you will have all the water you want to drink. If you drink the water in this jar, throw away this note." I don't think I need to expound upon that. The Apostle Paul said in 2 Corinthians 9:6, "Remember this: Whoever sows sparingly will also reap sparingly, and whoever sows generously will also reap generously." God is the One Who owns it all and distributes it all. It's not your business or your company. It's not your abilities or work ethic. It's not your brilliance or your charisma. It's God. It all begins with God. It all ends with God. And until we get that right, nothing else will work. Nothing.

You and I need to change our attitude. We need to say, "I'm willing to trust God and begin giving faithfully, systematically, and generously each week, so God can bless me out of my financial problems." And He will.

WHAT'S THE BEST WAY TO FINANCIAL FREEDOM?

You won't spend your way to financial freedom.

I've watched people get in financial difficulty, and they'll go out and buy a new car. Now how in the world do they do that? If you're already in financial difficulty, how does that work? Or they'll go buy new clothes. Or they'll go on some vacation. They'll say, "I just need to get away from it all." When you come back, it will all be waiting on you. It will all be there. And if you spent a lot of money, charging your vacation on little credit cards, there will be some big bills waiting for you when you get back. You won't spend your way to financial freedom.

You won't borrow your way to financial freedom.

"Well, all we need is a banker who has a great heart and

he'll give us a debt consolidation loan." Not long ago I talked to a friend of mine who used to serve as president of one of the banks in our city about debt consolidation loans. I wanted to reconfirm that I was giving the right advice to people because I never encourage people to get debt consolidation loans. To me, that's the absolute last straw. Why? Because unless you deal with the problem at the faucet, unless you turn it off first, it doesn't matter what kind of nice hose you have or what kind of attachments you have. If you don't stop the flow you still have tremendous pressure building up and sooner or later you'll be dealing with a flood.

So I asked my banker friend, "Does your bank do that?" He answered, "Yes, we do, but I'd want to sit down with those people and make sure they realize that's really not the source of the problem. That's the symptom."

The source of the problem is overspending. Living beyond your means. We've got to deal with that first. You won't borrow your way to financial freedom.

You won't cheat your way to financial freedom.

Someone will say, "What I'll do is, I'll just redo my taxes and keep some of the money the government is taking." Listen, if you do that, you're rebelling against Romans 13 where God says you need to obey the laws of the land. God up in heaven, Who determines your income and distributes wealth to you, is not going to honor the fact you're down here on earth cheating the IRS or anyone else.

You won't steal your way to financial freedom.

Someone says, "I know what I can do, I'll start adding a little bit of money to my expense reports each week. That way I'll get us some extra money." No you won't. You're not going to steal your way to financial freedom.

You won't beg your way to financial freedom.

Have you noticed all the people out on the highway holding cardboard signs or standing downtown with signs that say, "Will work for food?" They are lying and they know it. Sorry. I know you're probably thinking, "This guy doesn't have an ounce of compassion." No, I'm just telling you the truth. Check the newspaper from your city and you'll find all kinds of places looking for people to work. Right here in our own area *The Fort Worth Star-Telegram* has between six and ten pages of Want Ads offering jobs. Or you can get a copy of *The Dallas Morning News* and you'll find twice that many ads with people wanting to give people jobs.

After conducting a wedding recently, I did a little experiment. I went in all the restaurants close to our church—McDonald's, Burger King, Taco Bueno, and Denny's—and I asked, "Do you have any jobs available?" They looked at me kind of funny because I was dressed in a black suit and tie and they said, "Well, yes." And I said, "No, no, no, not for me. I just wanted to know if you had any jobs available." Every one of them had jobs available.

Here's my point: In the time it takes to go buy a magic marker and find a piece of cardboard for a sign, those people could've walked into McDonald's or someplace like it and said, "Could I work here?" and they'd gladly give them a job with benefits. They'll even give them a uniform to wear.

You're not going to beg your way to financial freedom. Someone says, "I'll just have my relatives pay." Listen, it's not your relatives' responsibility to take care of the fact you're a poor planner and a poor manager. I want to tell you something else. It's not the church's responsibility either. There are some people who believe the church ought to be this big, wonderful bucket of free money, and whenever people go out and overextend themselves or manage their money poorly, they erroneously believe the church ought to somehow give it away to anybody and everybody. (That's a subject for another book.)

You'd be shocked if you really studied what the Bible says about genuine benevolence. Did you know the Bible says if a person won't work, they're not supposed to eat? (Read 2 Thessalonians 3:10.) Did you know the Bible says the first people, the first support group that's supposed to take care of needy individuals are their own family members? (Read 1 Timothy 5:4-16.)

Be very careful when you start talking about benevolence and want to lay that burden on the doorsteps of the church. The first group that's supposed to support people is the immediate and extended family. And if they don't do it, the Bible says they're worse than unbelievers.

You won't gamble your way to financial freedom.

Someone says, "What I'm going to do is, I'm going to go buy a lottery ticket." I like to have fun with people who buy lottery tickets. When I go get gas at the Shell station, they're always in there. The Lottery-lovers. It never fails. No matter what time of day I go get gas, there's somebody in there buying lottery tickets, and I always say the same thing to them. They're standing in line and I say, "You know what? You might as well just take your money and throw it in that trash can over there." They turn and give me the weirdest looks.

"But, Preacher, if I won the lottery, I'd give that money to the church." We won't accept it. We will not accept money you got gambling. God in heaven wouldn't honor it. You say, "I'm going to win the lottery and I'm going to give all that money to the poor." That's who they're taking the money from in the first place to give to the winner! Statistics have proven the majority of people who purchase lottery tickets are those who can least afford it. God's not going to honor that. God won't bless that.

Someone else says, "I'm going to take this money and I'm going to go to Las Vegas." Now read this real slowly. You're going to take God's money. You're going to go to the devil's playground, and you're going to gamble it and make money for God and His kingdom? God's not going to honor that.

I've told people for years one of the reasons I don't buy lottery tickets is God would let me win. He would. I'd be the guy, if I went and bought a ticket, to win. You'd see it on the news. The reporter would say, "One ticket matched all 6 numbers or 7 numbers and it was bought in Arlington, Texas." And people in our church would say, "I wonder if it's somebody we know?" Then *The Star-Telegram* would have my picture on the front page the next morning, and it would say, "Pastor Barry Cameron won all this money." And you know what? The elders would say, "Hit the street, Jack." My credibility would be crushed. That's one reason I don't buy lottery tickets. Joseph said, "How could I do such a thing like this and disgrace my God." Wouldn't it be wonderful if Christians would start standing up for principle and truth and say, "I can't gamble, I need to honor and trust God. God's the One Who takes care of me, not the lottery and not the one-armed bandits in Las Vegas."

GENUINE SHARING

Several years ago at a conference I heard John Maxwell tell the story of a congressman who took his son to McDonald's. The father bought his son a Coke and a large order of fries and they went and sat down at one of those tables not built big enough for people to sit in. The father took a drink of his Coke and reached over to get a fry from his son, and his son put his hands around the fries and pulled them back. The father said, "That's okay, son." But as he sat there he started thinking to himself, "Doesn't my son realize I'm the one who gave him those fries in the first place? Doesn't he realize I can take those fries away from him any time I want? Doesn't he realize I can go up to the counter and I've got enough money I can buy all the fries I want? I can tell the people at the counter, 'Go out there and bury my son in French fries.' Doesn't my son realize I don't need any of his fries? I can go get my own. Doesn't he realize all I wanted to do was share a couple of fries with him?" And then the congressman said it hit him. His son was simply acting like he'd been acting with God.

Do you see any parallel? God blesses us and says, "I want to sit down with you and enjoy some of those blessings." So God sits down, and when He starts to come to us, we put our hands around all our stuff and say, "No, no, no, this is ours, God. We'll decide what we are going to give you." And God in Heaven says, "Don't they realize I'm the source of everything they've got? Don't they realize I have the power to take whatever blessings I've given them? Don't they realize I can bury them in blessings if I want to? Don't they realize I don't need anything they have? I just wanted to share it with them."

Don't make the mistake of thinking you can achieve financial success on your own and ignore the sovereignty of God. Those are His fries.

Read Proverbs 1:20-23. Wisdom is speaking and wisdom says, "I called out in the streets and no one would listen. Therefore, I will laugh at them when calamity comes" (paraphrase). Who is wisdom? Wisdom is literally God. God is saying, "I lay it out there. I tell My people here's what I want you to do, but if they won't listen what else can I do? They come running when they're in a mess, but what can I do? I tried to prevent it from ever happening by giving them the very principles that could've ensured their prosperity."

We're going to read about some phenomenal principles in

this book. But if we don't apply them to our lives, they won't do us any good. God wants to bless us, and He wants to prosper us, but we're the ones who decide whether it's going to happen or not.

The first step on the road to financial success is to change our attitude and acknowledge the sovereignty of God in our finances. "God, I want Your way. I want Your wisdom. I want Your guidance. I want to follow Your principles, and I want Your blessings in my life."

If you will make that commitment, you're already on your way to getting out of financial bondage and well on your way to financial success.

. . . from the G.O.O.D. file

(simple ideas to encourage you to Get Out Of Debt)

Getting into debt is easy. Getting out isn't. That's why it takes so much time, effort, and commitment. But if you'll invest in your future by doing what you ought to do now to get out of debt, you'll enjoy a multitude of dividends and benefits in the days ahead.

Trust in God, self-denial, and discipline are three major keys! We have to develop a nonnegotiable strategy when it comes to our finances. Just like the training regimen for an Olympic athlete that has to begin years before the actual event, we, too, have to discipline ourselves to do what we ought to do now if we want to be out of debt later.

But here's where the trouble begins. Some people are willing to pray and ask God for help, but that's where it ends. They want God to do it all and are unwilling to do anything themselves. Others start out great but get discouraged and give up. "It's too hard," they say.

Still others are unwilling to give up anything or deny themselves something now so they can enjoy everything later. "I'm going to enjoy life now," they say, little knowing that the more they enjoy (indulge) themselves now, the harder it will be to enjoy themselves in the future. The saying, "Play now and pay later, or pay now and play later," is certainly true when it comes to the stewardship of our finances.

Proverbs 24:27 says, "Finish your outdoor work and get your fields ready; after that, build your house." Translation: do what you ought to do first, then you can do what you want to do.

Action Plans

Getting out of debt will require us to:

A. Trust in God—He is the One Who gives you the ability to produce wealth. Start trusting Him alone for your finances.

B. Practice self-denial—Until you learn to control impulse spending and binge buying, you won't be able to get out of debt.

C. Be self-disciplined—No one else is going to do it for you. Learn to say no and go without those things you are tempted to buy.

If we'll do those three things on a consistent basis, over an extended period of time and not give up, the day will come when we can say, "I'm free forever from the bondage of debt!"

B Chapter 2
ondage

"Debt keeps you stuck in the trap of using your future to pay for your past."
—Mary Hunt

Let's review for a moment.

- We've already seen that the devil tries to deceive us into believing that all the church talks about is money.
- We learned that the devil tries to get us to believe money and things can satisfy us.
- We learned that the devil tries to convince us it's our money and we can do whatever we want with it.
- We learned that God is the One Who determines how much money we have.

- We learned that giving to God is the only way out of our financial problems.
- Whenever you see or hear the word INTEREST, I want you to immediately think of two other words: SOMEBODY ELSE. Because anytime you're paying interest, SOMEBODY ELSE is making money instead of you.
- Remember the French fry illustration with the congressman and his son? Don't ever forget, the French fries belong to God.

So the first step on the road to our financial success is to acknowledge the sovereignty of God, not only in our finances, but also in every area of our lives. Now we're ready to move to step two.

The second step on the road to financial success is: **We need to be aware of and avoid the subtlety of debt.**

THE BONDAGE OF DEBT

Not long ago in the course of one week I received five envelopes in the mail from credit card companies offering me new credit cards. One offered me, because of my "good credit standing," up to $50,000 on their card at 2.9% interest for the first nine months. One card said, because of my good credit standing, they'd give me $100,000 to spend. (On a credit card!) I told Mel Dietz, our administrator, "I could buy a car or a home with this."

Now not one of these five credit card company applications mentioned the word debt anywhere. In fact, some of those credit card applications said I could take balances from other credit cards and put it on theirs for an incredibly low 2.9% rate and everything would be fine.

I kept reading and when I got way down to the itsy-bitsy,

teeny-weeny, fine print, it said as long as I participated in their credit plan, things would be fine. But at the end of nine months the rate jumped to 16% on one, 22% on another. Honestly, that's the most ridiculous loan I could ever take out in my entire life.

Recently our local newspaper ran a full-page ad for a leading furniture company. I asked my wife, "What sticks out to you in this ad?" It said, "12 Months, No Interest." I saw the word interest, and what are the first two words that came to my mind? You're right: SOMEBODY ELSE! I read the ad and it said as long as you keep making the payments according to the company's revolving credit plan everything was fine.

WHAT CREDIT CARD COMPANIES DON'T WANT YOU TO KNOW

Don't miss this. Remember the word "revolving." The credit card companies call good credit people, in other words, people who use their credit cards regularly and only pay the monthly payment required, "revolvers." (Sounds like something that, when loaded, can be dangerous, doesn't it? Just a thought.)

Credit card companies want you, me, and everybody in the world to be a "revolver." If they can get us to be "revolvers," people who will just keep making the minimum payment each month and keep revolving that debt over and over again, they can make a lot of money off us. They love "revolvers."

Guess what they call people like me who pay their credit cards off and never keep a balance that rolls over to the next month? This is the absolute truth. They call people like me "deadbeats." If you pay your credit card off each month, the credit card industry considers you a deadbeat! I'd call you a genius, but we'll get into that later.

So I read the whole ad, saw this beautiful furniture, and read this "12 months, no interest," offer. I went to the bottom of the ad to the ultrasmall, fine print, and it said, "at any point if you fail to make your minimum monthly payment, the interest rate goes to 21%." Just like that. Again, the ad didn't mention debt anywhere on the page.

Debt is subtle and those who try to encourage us to get into debt are subtle themselves and sometimes even sinister as well. That's why we need to always read the fine print before we foolishly pursue debt of any amount.

GOD'S WILL IS FOR US TO BE DEBT FREE

In Deuteronomy 28 we find some incredibly sound financial advice. I'll tell you right up front that I believe without a shadow of a doubt that it's God's will for us to be debt free.

Look at these verses beginning in Deuteronomy 28:12: "The LORD will open the heavens, the storehouse of his bounty, to send rain on your land in season and to bless all the work of your hands. You will lend to many nations but will borrow from none." Now God doesn't say borrowing is wrong. Don't read that into the verse; nowhere does it say borrowing is wrong. But He says, "You're going to live in such a way (God's people) that you'll lend to other nations and you'll borrow from no one." That's His plan. The next verse says, "The LORD will make you the head and not the tail. If you pay attention to the commands of the LORD your God that I give you this day and carefully follow them, you will always be at the top, never at the bottom. Do not turn aside from any of the commands I give you today, to the right or to the left, following other gods and serving them."

It's very clear. God does not want us to be in debt. He wants us to be "lenders" instead of "borrowers." Unfortunately the majority of people in the Christian community are seriously and severely in debt.

"Lenders and not borrowers" doesn't describe the average church in America. It doesn't describe the average Christian either. Yet God said, "I want you to be free so you can lend to many and borrow from none." Do I have your attention?

I received an e-mail back in December of 1999 from one of our church members. I asked permission to share it. It said,

> I for one am looking forward to your January series on being debt free. Paul and I have been totally debt free since February 25, 1997. That was when we made the last payment on our house. We had a 30-year loan, paid it off in 7 years, and it is a great feeling. We feel the Lord has been very good to us. I still like hearing things on finances and debt because I still learn things.[1]

I received another e-mail the same week from another family in our church and asked permission to share theirs.

> I wanted to thank you for your powerful message today. My wife and I have been visiting the church for awhile now and are signed up for the Membership Class on the 9th. Your message on getting out of debt became a reality to us about eight years ago. We both fell under conviction about this and resolved to become totally debt free. Well, we have as of several years ago now. I can only attempt to say one does not fully understand the yoke one is under until they are free. We will never go back to that bondage.[2]

That's exactly what I want to deal with in this chapter: The bondage of debt. If I do my job correctly in these next few pages, you will never, ever again be able to look at the word "debt" or hear the word "debt" and not get a sick feeling in your stomach. I want to teach you to hate debt. I want to help you get to the place where, when you see the word, or hear somebody talking about it that you'll just say to yourself (and perhaps them as well), "I hate debt." Because one of the most important factors on the road to financial success is having a proper understanding of the bondage of debt.

Have you ever stopped to consider what it would be like to be completely out of debt? Have you ever imagined what life would be like if you didn't owe a dime or a dollar to anyone? Have you ever dreamed about that? Have you ever thought, "If this coming Friday I could get my paycheck and it wasn't pre-obligated to anybody or anyone and I could do anything I wanted with it, what would life be like?" (Made you feel good, didn't I?)

Just the thought of being out of debt gives you a great feeling. Why? Because you weren't created to live in bondage to anyone or anything.

Listen carefully because I want to explain something. Your entire life would be absolutely different than what it is right now if you were out of debt. We all know it would sure be nice to get there, but some people aren't willing to make the decisions and develop the disciplines it takes to get there. Like an Olympic athlete who wants to participate in the Olympics but spends every morning of his life at the donut shop. Sorry, it's not going to happen. It's not going to work out. You might have a great dream. But if you're nibbling on chocolate-covered, cream-filled donuts every morning, the chances of your even attending the Olympics are slim.

Just think of the possibilities if you were totally and completely debt free. Think for a moment what would happen at your church. Can you imagine what your church could do if everyone in your church were debt free? (Made you feel good again, didn't I?)

Think what your church could do if all of the people in your church were totally and completely debt free. Can you imagine a missionary visiting and he shares with one of the ushers, "I'm on my way to Brazil. They routed our flight through here and it got delayed last night. So I can't fly out until this afternoon. I'd always heard about your church and wanted to come and worship with you. So I'm here today."

The usher says to the missionary, "What are you going to be doing in Brazil?" The missionary answers, "I'm going down there to try to be an encouragement to them, train some preachers, and to help build a building." So the usher says, "What will you need to do all that?" And the missionary replies, "We're praying God will give us $100,000." So the usher says, "Go ahead and go on into the service and I'll get back with you."

The usher goes to the church administrator and says, "We've got a visiting missionary with us today and he needs $100,000 to go to Brazil. Wouldn't it be a great idea if we helped him out?" The administrator checks with a few elders and goes back and gets the pastor and says, "We'd like for you to make a small announcement at the end of the service and see if we can help this missionary out."

Now follow me. As astounding as what I am about to tell you is going to appear, it's absolutely possible. If the people in your church were out of debt, you could give that fellow not only $100,000, you could probably receive an offering for $400,000. Someone says, "Oh my goodness. What would we do with the extra $300,000?" Give it to the missionary. What a blessing that would be. And no one would have to sacrifice because you were debt free.

Regrettably the reality in most churches is that they probably can't do something like that this coming Sunday morning. You know why? Because the average church in America and the average church member in America is so miserably in debt that if they received an offering at the close of the regular Sunday service, it would more likely be $4,000.

Tell me which scenario does a better job honoring God? We need to get out of debt. If you can't think of enough reasons in your own heart and life to want to get out of debt, let that be a motivation to you. To be a part of a church where there wouldn't be a single need that couldn't be met, including visiting missionaries who need $100,000.

I've been praying for years to be a part of a church that could give $1 million to missions in one calendar year. But you know what I'm praying now? I believe one of the reasons God burdened me to help get our church out of debt is so we can receive a $1 million offering for missions in one day. Yes, you read it right: in one day. Now we're not going to be able to do it next week, but I do believe we will get to the place where that will happen.

If every member of our church were out of debt, it wouldn't take any sacrifice at all to receive a one-day offering of one million dollars. But in most churches, if you started talking like that, people would start getting nervous because an offering of that magnitude for missions in one day is unheard of and would take considerable sacrifice. But it shouldn't make anyone nervous at all.

What I'm trying to get you to do is to get a visual picture. And the picture I'm wanting you to see is that your life and your church are being seriously and drastically affected because of debt. Miserable, worthless, ridiculous, life-killing, happiness-destroying debt. Do you get the picture yet?

I think you already know God doesn't want His church to be that way. In fact, Peter Wagner wrote a book called *Churchquake,* and in it he tells the story of two churches and these are his words: "These churches seem to have all the money they need to accomplish whatever they perceive God is calling them to do. They are both out of debt."[3] Listen to this: "Crenshaw Christian Center is an African-American church in the inner city of Los Angeles pastored by Fred Price. When they outgrew their building on Crenshaw Avenue, they purchased the old Pepperdine University Campus and built the Faith Dome, a worship center that has 10,146 theater seats. The total cost was $26 million: $14 million for the land, $12 million for the building."[4]

Dr. Wagner was invited to be their guest for the three-hour dedication service. And he said that the grand finale of their dedication service, the first service in the new building, was when Fred Price took a letter out of his pocket from the Security Pacific bank and it read, "Paid in full."

Lakewood Church in Houston, Texas, pastored by Joel Osteen is another example. It's a multi-ethnic church, begun in 1959 with 234 people. After a number of building programs to accommodate their continual growth, in 1986, they had 5,000 members. They had thought about moving to a more affluent part of the city, but God told them to build out where they were in a deteriorating community in Northeast Houston. In 1986, with Houston in the middle of a deep recession and the oil crisis having erupted, the city entered a period of economic collapse, when businesses and individuals were going bankrupt. Just two months after Pastor Osteen had undergone open-heart surgery, the church built a new 8,000-seat sanctuary and moved in it in one year, debt free.[5]

Let me insert this little thought: Did you hear all the bad stuff that was going on? The economy was bad, businesses were going bankrupt, the preacher just had open-heart surgery, and none of that mattered. Why? The people are debt free.

"In 1992, they built a $6 million family-life center and office building. It was finished in one year and paid for in cash without taking one special offering."[6] That's the way God wants His church to be. That's Deuteronomy 28. "You will lend to many nations but borrow from none."

There's an outstanding book called *Debt-Free Living* by Larry Burkett. If you don't have it, you need to get it. Listen to what he says: "Regardless of how it seems today, debt is not normal in any economy and should not be normal for God's people. We live in a debt-ridden society that is now virtually dependent on a constant expansion of credit to keep the economy going. That is a symptom of a society no longer willing to follow God's directions."[7]

Not long ago our church Administrator, Mel Dietz, and I were out looking for one of those radio/tape player/TVs to give to one of the missionaries our church supports. So we were going around to stores and we bought one. By the way, we paid cash for it. (You've got to practice what you preach.) We even got the batteries to go with it!

When we were out driving around, Mel said, "You would've thought it was Christmas at all these stores today." I agreed and added, "Look at all these vehicles. You know people are miserably in debt and there they go, walking into the store, to get even more miserably in debt. Then they'll walk into a church like ours on Sunday, and we'll say we've got a missionary from Brazil who has a need and they'll respond, "Oh, all that church wants is my money." We both laughed. But it really isn't funny when you think about it.

Isn't it sad how that works? The devil leads us into debt so he can keep us in bondage and keep us from doing great things for God and His kingdom.

DOES THE BIBLE FORBID GOING INTO DEBT?

No. But it sure discourages us from going into debt. Let me give you some Biblical principles. I'll share seven of them from the Bible.

Seven Biblical Principles about Debt

1. Going into debt makes you a servant to someone else other than God. In Proverbs 22:7 Solomon says, "The rich rule over the poor, and the borrower is servant to the lender." When you borrow, instead of God being your Lord and God being your boss, somebody else is calling the shots. Let me warn you, when you're not able to make the payments, they'll start calling some shots you don't want to hear.

2. It's clearly a sin if you borrow and don't repay. That's very clear in the Bible. Psalm 37:21 says, "The wicked borrow and do not repay, but the righteous give generously." Whenever I see the Bible says, "the righteous give generously," the reason I believe they can give generously is, they're out of debt.

3. The Bible warns that it's better not to go into debt. You're not going to believe this verse. Proverbs 17:18 says, "A man lacking in judgment strikes hands in pledge and puts up security for his neighbor." I read that in the NIV and thought it sounded weird. It sounds like you and me going into debt for our neighbors. So I did some checking on it and guess what the literal translation of the Hebrew is? It says, "The man lacking in judgment strikes hands in pledge, makes an agreement for debt in the presence of his neighbor." Makes a whole lot of difference, doesn't it? It's not the fact that I'm going into debt for my neighbor. That would almost seem as if I was being a Good Samaritan, doing something nice for my neighbor. But that's not what it's talking about. It's saying a man lacking in judgment, a foolish man, goes into debt, and his neighbor knows about it.

I can't wait for my neighbors to drive up and down our street. We might not have the nicest cars in the neighborhood or the nicest house, but they're all going to know our house and our cars are paid for. People drive by our church and look at our facilities and our grounds, and they may not understand all the different buildings and what they're used for, but we want them to know they're all paid for.

4. The longest term of debt God's people took on in the Bible was seven years. In Deuteronomy 15:1 God says, "At the end of every seven years you must cancel debts." Now I know some of you will read that and say, "That would be great. That would be wonderful." Keep reading. "This is how it is to be done: Every creditor shall cancel the loan he has made to his fellow Israelite." Now it's interesting, God doesn't say he should have never made the loan in the first place, but He says, "Now is the time you should cancel it."

The Bible doesn't forbid borrowing. The Bible doesn't forbid debt. It just says there's a whole lot better way to live without it. Keep reading.

> He shall not require payment from his fellow Israelite or brother, because the LORD'S time for canceling debts has been proclaimed. You may require payment from a foreigner, but you must cancel any debt your brother owes you. However, there should be no poor among you, for in the land the LORD your God is giving you to possess as your inheritance, he will richly bless you, if only you fully obey the LORD your God and are careful to follow all these commands I am giving you today. For the LORD your God will bless you as he has promised, and you will lend to many nations but will borrow from none. You will rule over many nations but none will rule over you.

5. You are not in control of your own future. James 4:13-15 says, "Now listen, you who say, 'Today or tomorrow we will go to this or that city, spend a year there, carry on business and make money.' Why, you do not even know what will happen tomorrow. What is your life? You are a mist that appears for a little while and then vanishes." You don't know that you're going to have more money down the road to pay for what you're going into debt for. You can't possibly know that. But the salesman will tell you you can.

Several years ago I bought a Toyota Starlet. They don't

even make them anymore. It wasn't much bigger than a bicycle. Honestly, it's the smallest car I'd ever seen. (Like a go-cart with doors.) But it was all I could afford. The salesman's name, I'll never forget it, was Hank Williams. No, he didn't sing, but he gave me quite a song and told me, "This is a good starter car for you." What he didn't know was it wasn't a starter car for me. I'd already had six or seven. But I'd gotten so miserably in debt that it was all I could afford. He said, "You know, you'll come back here in a couple years and you're going to be so flush with cash. You're going to get that Toyota Supra right there. I can put you in that thing. Man, you're going to make so much money." Unfortunately what he said never happened. But remember, he was a salesman. He was already talking me into the fact that I needed to come back and buy that bigger car because I was going to be making more money. We don't know that. We're not in control of our own future. We have no guarantees.

6. When you go into debt you are asking someone else other than God to meet your needs. That's very dangerous. Paul said in Philippians 4:19, "And my God will meet all your needs according to his glorious riches in Christ Jesus." When we go into debt, we are trusting First National Bank or First Security or the Credit Union or whatever the name of your bank is instead of God.

7. When you go into debt and mortgage your future, you affect your whole family. In Proverbs 11:28-29 Solomon says, "Whoever trusts in his riches will fall, but the righteous will thrive like a green leaf. He who brings trouble on his family will inherit only wind, and the fool will be servant to the wise."

I think it's pretty clear in the Bible: Debt is not a good thing for us and does not represent God's perfect will for our lives.

DEFINITIONS FOR DEBT

Let me give you a couple of definitions for debt. This will help you have the right attitude toward debt. 1) Debt is a: Dumb Explanation for Buying Things. D-E-B-T. 2) If you have to use debt to buy something (D-E-B-T), think of these words: Don't Even Buy That.

Now remember, when you see the word "interest," I want you to think of two words: SOMEBODY ELSE, and when you think of debt, here's what I want you to think of: Been there, done with that. It's a dumb excuse for buying things. I'm not going to do it anymore.

There's a book out by Mary Hunt called *Debt-Proof Living*. Mary says, "For fun, I looked up the word debt in my trusty Thesaurus. Here's what it said: Debt—obligation, encumbrance, in the red, pound of flesh, arrears, inability to pay, bilked, bound, beholden, up to one's ears, over one's head, mortgaged to the hilt, in the poverty trap, unable to keep the wolf from the door, hard-up, beaten down, financially embarrassed, strapped, stripped, fleeced, busted."[8]

Are you getting the picture about debt yet? It's not good. In fact, Mary Hunt says there's only five things you can do with money:

1. **You can give it.** (That's the top of her list. Mine, too!)
2. **You can save it.**
3. **You can invest it.**
4. **You can lend it.**
5. **You can spend it.**[9]

There are only five things you can do with your money. So why blow it by getting in debt and losing it through paying interest to somebody else? It makes no sense whatsoever.

You may be sitting there reading this and saying, "I don't know if I can ever get out of debt." Can you get out of debt?

Absolutely. Regardless of who you are. Regardless of how much debt you're in. I just hope you're not one of these people who walks around saying, "My dad was always in debt. My grandfather was always in debt." If I had the time, I'd debate that statement with you. Because when you go back to the time when people lived who are your grandfather's age and your great-grandfather's age, you'll quickly discover they didn't live lives of debt. They paid for things with cash. They were smarter than we are. Something else you may not know about those "good old days," they didn't have to lock their doors at night and they could leave the keys in their cars overnight. Now everything's changed, and not necessarily for the better. I believe anybody can get out of debt if they really want to and are willing to do what it takes to get out of debt.

According to the Theory of Aerodynamics as demonstrated through wind tunnel tests, the bumblebee can't fly. Scientifically, aerodynamically, the bumblebee cannot fly. All the math, all the science says the bumblebee cannot fly because of its size, its weight, the shape of its body in relation to its total wing spread. Flying is scientifically impossible. But the bumblebee doesn't pay attention to science and math or the Theory of Aerodynamics. The bumblebee, being totally ignorant of scientific theory, goes ahead and flies anyway and makes honey everyday.

You can get out of debt, you just have to want to, and you have to be willing to do what it takes to get there.

HOW DO YOU GET OUT OF DEBT?

1. **Make the irrevocable commitment to God and to yourself that you're going to get out of debt.**

Make an irrevocable commitment, "I am going to get out of debt." Make that commitment to God first, make it to yourself, and then share it with as many other people as you can so they can hold you accountable. If they see you pull in the driveway with a brand new Lincoln two weeks after you said you were going to get out of debt, they're going to say, "Uh, wait a minute." We need that kind of accountability to be successful.

2. Don't take on any more debt.

Just say, "That's it. I'm not borrowing anything else. I'm not going into debt." If you have to use debt to buy something, say to yourself, "Don't even buy that." It's a dumb explanation for buying things.

3. Put God first in your giving.

By the way, that doesn't mean you just throw God a bone every week, a little dollar or whatever change you've got in your pocket. The Bible teaches emphatically, as a minimum, that each of us should tithe the first 10% or our income back to God. Our first fruits belong to God. If we're not doing that, we'll never get out of debt.

4. Develop a written plan.

Some people don't like the word budget. I do a lot of counseling, especially premarital counseling and marriage counseling. Every time I counsel people, we end up talking about financial problems and I talk about budgets. Couples will say to me, "Oh yeah, it's a good thing to have a budget." And I always ask, "Do you have one?" In almost every case they'll answer, "Well, no, we're working on that."

Get a budget. My wife and I have a five-page budget. I can tell you from personal experience that it's one of the secrets to getting out of debt and staying out of debt. One of the first things you need to do is to get an accurate picture in print (in black and white) of what a mess you're in. That's where you need to start. It's not fun. It's not a full-blown party writing down all those bills and all those obligations, seeing you have a whole lot more going out than you have coming in. But you need to do that. That's where budgeting starts.

Our five-page budget shows how much our income is, what our bills are, what our obligations are, what's in savings, what's in retirement. On a weekly basis my wife and I both know every dime we have and every responsibility we have. We have a list of which bills are coming next week and which ones need to be paid. It's incredibly helpful and informative. It's not hard. It's not rocket science. It's common sense.

You don't have to be a great mathematician to have a budget, but you need to have a written plan. You need to see what's really happening in your finances. By the way, as long as you have debt, you don't have true savings. You need to know that. It's good to have savings. I encourage you to do that. But just remember, as long as you have debt, you don't really have savings. Especially if you're earning interest of 4% on your savings and yet you're still paying off credit card debts that carry an interest rate of between 19-21%.

5. Set an attainable timeframe to get out of debt.

Christian financial expert Larry Burkett says anyone can be out of debt in seven years. But you may say, "I don't know; that might be too much pressure." Then put eight years down. But set a time. Set a goal. "We're going to be debt free by a certain day." If you don't set a goal, you'll never do it.

Several years ago there was a fellow sitting in my home and he was quite a bit overweight. We were both sitting there eating some dessert and he started telling me how he was going to lose weight. I thought, "Now isn't this funny. Here we are eating dessert, and you're talking about losing weight." But isn't that the way we are? We lay in bed and watch people working out on TV. We see those rock-hard abs and say, "Yeah, that's what I'm going to be like." Then we go downstairs and get a bowl of ice cream and a plate of cookies.

There has to be a goal or you're going to be in the same position or even worse by this time next year. You need to say, "I'm going to do this," and you're going to have to go without some things and make some changes in your lifestyle.

6. Adjust your lifestyle.

You don't have to go out to eat everyday. Let me tell you, the worst investment you make on a daily basis is paying $1.50 for iced tea or soda. It only costs them 5 to 7 cents. So they love it when you come in and say, "Oh yes, I'll have a large root beer." Sure, no problem. As they walk away, they're saying, "Profit, profit, profit." Then they'll ask, "Would you like to start with an appetizer?" You know what a starter is for a restaurant? More money for them. You say, "Well, if I took a sack lunch to work, people would make fun of me." That's fine. Let them make fun of you until you're out of debt and then they'll come and ask, "How did you do that sack lunch deal? Can you teach me how to get out of debt?"

You don't have to go out to dinner every Friday night. You don't have to go out to movies. You don't have to stop and always get something at the store. Some people go to the mall on a weekly basis and they can't walk out unless they have a bag in their hands. Let me give you a suggestion. Go to the mall today, walk the whole length of it, get in your car, and go home with nothing in your hand. Trust me. It will make you feel good. You can say, "I did it, I did it. I walked around the mall and didn't have to buy anything."

I love books. But I learned a long time ago, sometimes it's good for me to walk into a bookstore pick up a bunch of books, handle them, put them down, and walk out just to prove I'm still in control. That bookstore doesn't own me.

You'll never get out of debt if you don't adjust your lifestyle. There will always be people who make fun of you.

There will always be people who don't understand you. And that's all right. When our family first made the decision to get out of debt, my son came to me and said, "Dad, you know there's some people making fun of you?" I said, "Yeah. So what?" He said, "Dad, I still think you're doing what's right." I said, "Son, I know I am. One of these days we're going to be debt free and they won't be making fun of us anymore."

You can't let the critics and the people who make fun of you rule your life. That's one of the reasons we're in debt and in a mess now. We listen to other people who said this is a good deal, try this, get that, buy this. We don't have to have what they have or buy what they tell us to buy. We need to get out of debt and then it won't matter what they say. In fact, they'll probably come to you and ask if you'd be willing to help them get out of debt.

7. Begin to systematically pay off all your debts.

You need to have a *written* plan. You need to look at your obligations and then you need to start paying them off. I recommend you pay the smallest ones off first. Then use the money that used to go for those to pay for the next largest one.

Some people say, "Well, you need to pay off the highest interest rate first." If you do the math, you'll figure out it doesn't work any better than if you just pay off the smallest one first. Start with the smallest one and, I assure you, if you've got a written plan, and you're able to cross one off, "That debt's gone," it will give you encouragement and momentum to get after the other obligations and eventually enable you to get out of debt.

Someone wrote these words called "It Can't Be Done."

> The ones who miss all the fun
>   are those who say it can't be done.
> In solemn pride they stand aloof
>   and greet each venture with reproof.

> Had they the power to face
> > the history of the human race.
> We'd have no radio or motor cars,
> > no streets lit by electric stars.
> No telegraph or telephone.
> > We'd linger in the age of stone.
> The world would sleep if things were run
> > by those who say, "It can't be done."

It can be done. And I want to encourage you: I'm committed to raising up an army of people who are absolutely, completely, and permanently debt free. I'm absolutely committed to it. You can do it. *Everyone* can do it.

Not only can it be done, it will be done. With God's help and for God's glory we can all be debt free. As I said earlier in this chapter, I believe there's no question God wants us out of debt. And I believe there's no question God is willing to do whatever it takes to get us out of debt. You know how I know that? You and I entered this world in debt to sin. And God knew that wasn't good. So He sent His own Son to pay off the debt we could never pay in order that we could be free. John 8:36 says, "So if the Son sets you free, you will be free indeed." There's no freedom and certainly no feeling in the world like being free from the debt of sin. The next best feeling is to be free from the debts of this world. God will help you with those, too!

. . . from the G.O.O.D. file

(simple ideas to encourage you to Get Out Of Debt)

Three Essentials to Getting Out of Debt

1. What you SAY. If you continually say, "We'll never get out of debt," GUESS WHAT? You won't. The Bible says, "As a man thinks in his heart, so is he." You've got to change your conversation. Start thanking God for helping you get out of debt and continually tell your spouse, your family, and your friends, "Not only can we do it (get out of debt), we're going to do it." And watch what happens.

2. What you SPEND. If you continually overspend your income, you'll never get out of debt. You have to change your spending habits. Here are some ideas of things you can control: going out to eat, magazine and newspaper subscriptions, long distance phone calls, electricity, cell phone calls, buying new clothes, etc. Your debts and the interest you have to pay on them will continue to control your life and your future until you get your spending under control.

3. What you SAVE. Resist the urge to splurge. Don't spend everything you earn. Try to make it through every week with something left over you can save, even if it's only $5. You don't have to see the newest movie that just came out. You don't have to have the latest CD or DVD. Postpone those types of pleasures and put the money in savings. You'll quickly realize the folly of impulse purchases and the security that comes from having a nest egg of any size drawing interest for you in the bank.

Take some G.O.O.D. advice, watch what you SAY, what you SPEND, and what you SAVE. It'll help you get out of debt!

Action Plans

A. Post your commitment to get out of debt in a visible place. It will keep you motivated daily.

B. Cut one of your frivolous expenses from your budget. Replace it with a free equivalent.

C. If your employer will do this, see if you can get part of your paycheck automatically deposited in a savings account every month. It's one way to force yourself to save.

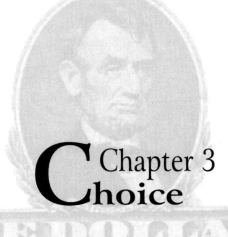

C Chapter 3
Choice

*"When we eat out, most of us expect to tip
the waiter or waitress 15 percent.
When we suggest 10 percent as a minimum church offering,
some folks are aghast."*
—Felix A. Lorenz, Jr.

Many people try to laugh away their financial problems or smile and act like everything's okay. Truth is, there's nothing funny about having financial problems. Having had more than my fair share of them, I think I can say with some degree of authority there's nothing funny about financial problems or financial stress. So why put on a charade for others and act like nothing's wrong?

Someone wisely said, "Too often we spend money we don't have for things we don't need to impress people we don't even know." Someone else said, "When our outgo exceeds our income, then our upkeep will become our downfall." There's nothing fun about living with financial pressure and stress. There's nothing inherently humorous or enjoyable about living with bills, burdens, and the bondage of debt. Yet the majority of people live under the bondage of continual financial problems, financial stress, and miserable debt. I think it's a rather sad commentary on our society.

WHO'S BEHIND YOUR FINANCIAL PROBLEMS?

Before we can solve our financial problems, we need to find out who's behind them. Who's responsible for the financial mess we're in? When you get the answer, you're going to be shocked. Once we know who's behind our financial problems, then we're going to discover how we can solve them. Now make no mistake about it; you have a very significant role in your own financial problems through the choices you make. But there's somebody else behind your financial problems, and it's not your wife and it's not your husband.

If you study the Scriptures, it's very clear the devil wants you and me to be up to our ears in financial problems. He wants us to be up to our eyeballs in financial trouble, but even he's not the one responsible for our financial problems.

The shocking reality is, God is the One Who's behind our financial problems. Yes, you read it right. Almighty God! Here's the irony of it all: you and I can get out of our financial problems anytime we want. Literally, we can get out of our financial difficulties and get out from under the stress of our financial problems any time we want to. But we have to choose to do it *God's way*.

Personal Choice

Some will be shocked to read this statement, but no one is predestined to live his or her life in financial trouble. Have you ever known people who always seem to have cars that break down? Ever known people who always seem to have a major crisis going on at their house? Last week it was the dishwasher that blew up. Last month it was the washer that went bad. The month before that one of their kids was in a car wreck, and they just seem to have one financial calamity after another. It's so easy for us to look at them and say, "Well, they're just one of those people predestined to have financial problems their whole life." Where did you hear that? The Bible doesn't teach that anyone is predestined to be in financial trouble their entire life. We have the power to choose. You and I can choose to have a life that is drastically different from the life others choose.

I took my son to a Doc Severinsen concert in Fort Worth one night. Yes, he found the money in his budget to go, paid for his own ticket, and even bought our dinner. As we walked out of Wendy's (I know it's not the best restaurant in Fort Worth), I said, "Thanks, son, for dinner." (That's got a nice ring to it, don't you think?) We went to the concert and the average age of the people had to be sixty years and older. They were all dressed in coats and ties and nice dresses. We weren't dressed up quite that nice. We were sitting in the upper box level and as we looked around I said, "Matt, are any of your friends here, any of the other guys you know who play trumpet?" He said, "No, they're not here." And I said, "Well, it's great that you come to concerts like this because when you're exposed to things like this, it raises your sights and your vision for what you can do." (My son is quite a trumpet player with a whole wall of awards.)

As we sat there, I tried to encourage him. I told him, "If you'll always do what others don't, you'll always get what other's won't." And that's true for finances. If you'll make the right choices in your life and do what other people are not willing to do, if you'll be willing to follow God and trust Him when it comes to finances, you'll get in your life what other people never experience. The tragedy is, more often than not, the financial problems that come in our lives are merely the result of our making wrong choices.

Consequences of Selfishness

In Haggai 1:1 (there's a book you don't hear much about!) we discover some people experiencing a number of problems. And get this, the problems were a direct result of their ignoring God. Specifically, ignoring the things of God and, even worse, the house of God. They were putting their own desires first and ignoring God. Watch the problems they get into. Verses 1-2 say, "In the second year of King Darius, on the first day of the sixth month, the word of the LORD came through the prophet Haggai to Zerubbabel son of Shealtiel, governor of Judah, and to Joshua son of Jehozadak, the high priest: This is what the LORD Almighty says: 'These people say, "The time has not yet come for the LORD'S house to be built."'"

Keep that in mind. They'd made a decision. "It's not time to do anything for God yet." Now watch this. "Then the word of the LORD came through the prophet Haggai: 'Is it a time for you yourselves to be living in your paneled houses, while this house remains a ruin?'" (You and I think of paneled houses and don't think they are very nice. But it was nice back then. In fact, they were considered quite nice.)

So God says, "Is it right for you to be living in these lavish, luxurious homes while this house, My house, remains a ruin?" Verse 5 says, "Now this is what the LORD Almighty says: 'Give careful thought to your ways.'" Watch what's about to happen. The financial problems are going to start piling up.

"'You have planted much, but have harvested little. You eat, but never have enough. You drink, but never have your fill. You put on clothes, but are not warm. You earn wages, only to put them in a purse with holes in it.'"

Like little gerbils in a cage going around in a circle. It doesn't matter what they do, nothing changes. They work harder, plant more seed, do more stuff, and yet it seems as if they have nothing and aren't getting anywhere. (Remind you of anyone you know?) Something's going on here. Wouldn't you agree?

Look at verse 7: "This is what the LORD Almighty says: 'Give careful thought to your ways. Go up into the mountains and bring down timber and build the house [God's house], so that I may take pleasure in it and be honored.'" Sometimes I run into people who say, "Well, there shouldn't be any church buildings and there shouldn't be any church facilities. We ought to give all that money to missions." I wonder if these people even have a Bible to read, and if they do, have they ever read it? The most phenomenal facility ever constructed on the face of the earth was the temple for which God had given the blueprint. God's the One Who said, "Build Me a house." He says, "Build Me a house so that I may take pleasure in it and be honored." Now watch verse 9, "You expected much, but see, it turned out to be little."

Get the picture? They worked hard, strategized well, and planned carefully. They said, "We're going to be all right. We're going to have a great harvest. Things are going to be great. Everything's going to be wonderful." But in verse 9 God says, "What you brought home, I blew away."

Have you ever gone home and opened up your wallet or pocketbook and said, "Where has my money gone?" Did you know the Bible says money has wings? The Bible says it can fly away. The book of Proverbs says, don't feast your eyes on riches and don't get too attached to riches because they can fly away like a bird (Proverbs 23:5).

"'Why?' declares the LORD Almighty. 'Because of my house, which remains a ruin, while each of you is busy with his own house.'" Here's the key: they got their priorities all out of order. "Therefore," God says, "because of you the heavens have withheld their dew and the earth its crops. I called for a drought on the fields and the mountains, on the grain, the new wine, the oil and whatever the ground produces, on men and cattle, and on the labor of your hands."

God says, "You have your priorities all messed up. You put yourself first and not Me. So I shut it all down." I want to make something crystal clear for you. God has the power to do that. And when you and I get our priorities out of order, when we put other things or ourselves first, before Him, He'll shut us down. Our financial problems are merely the result of God trying to get our attention. I can guarantee you, every time you and I put ourselves first and put God last, we're headed for trouble. Every time.

Financial problems are to you and your family, your business, and even your church, just like pain sensors in your physical body. God has equipped your physical body with pain sensors. They are there to keep you from destroying your body. God has put pain sensors in my hand so if I hit a wall hard enough, those pain sensors will say, "Don't do that again, dummy!" My brain will say to my hand, "What on earth were you thinking?" My hand will say, "I'm not supposed to think, I'm just a hand." Those pain sensors are God given to keep us from hurting ourselves. Because of His infinite wisdom and because He loves us, God has put pain sensors in our body to keep us from destroying our body. Like the warning lights on the dashboard of your car. Pay attention to those warning lights!

Years ago when I was dating my wife, I was driving her car

home from Missouri to Tulsa, Oklahoma, when the warning lights started flashing on the dashboard. I drove several miles ignoring the warning light, thinking everything would be all right. By the time I'd pulled over, the engine was blown. It cost us hundreds of dollars to get it fixed because I didn't pay attention to a little warning light on the dashboard that was trying to tell me, "There's a problem, there's a problem, slow down, get off the road, get help!"

Pain Sensors

Warning lights, pain sensors, and financial problems are all designed to get our attention and help us avoid unnecessary trouble. The most insidious disease known to the human body is not cancer and it's not AIDS. The worst disease the body can get is leprosy. Because it systematically destroys all the pain sensors in your body so you can literally run your hand through a wall and not feel it.

Let me tell you what I think is one of the deadliest financial diseases people get: credit. What leprosy is to the human body, credit is to our finances. Credit tells us everything's okay no matter what we do. We may be destroying ourselves, destroying our future, and destroying ourselves financially, but we keep getting these notices in the mail raising our credit limit, telling us we're such wonderful people and can go out and borrow the world. I believe financial problems are God's way of saying to us, "You're not on the right path."

In fact, in Hebrews 12:6 the Bible says He (God) disciplines us because he loves us. God is not about to let you and me walk in rebellion and disobedience and get away with it. So He shuts us down. He gives us financial problems.

Blessings of Obedience

Let me show you another verse: Malachi 3:9. Now remember, in Haggai 1 God is the One behind the problems.

Now here in Malachi notice that God is the One behind the blessings.

Do you see the difference? In Haggai 1 the problems were a direct result of the people ignoring God, specifically the house of God, and putting themselves first. But now in Malachi 3 the blessings are the direct result of people putting God first and tithing. Notice what it says in verses 8-9: "Will a man rob God?" (That's not a very smart thing to do, by the way.) "Yet you rob me. But you ask, 'How do we rob you?' In tithes and offerings. You are under a curse—the whole nation of you—because you are robbing me."

God had shut everything down. In Malachi 3:10, He gives them the answer to getting out of their problems. He says, "'Bring the whole tithe into the storehouse, that there may be food in my house. Test me in this,' says the LORD Almighty, 'and see if I will not throw open the floodgates of heaven and pour out so much blessing that you will not have room enough for it.'" Now watch verses 11-12, "'I will prevent pests from devouring your crops, and the vines in your fields will not cast their fruit,' says the LORD Almighty. 'Then all the nations will call you blessed, for yours will be a delightful land,' says the LORD Almighty."

Don't miss this. God is in control. He's either the One behind our financial problems or the One behind our blessings. And guess who chooses which One He's going to be in our lives? You and I.

Old versus New Testament

Some will undoubtedly say, "That's Old Testament stuff and, Pastor, we don't need to waste our time on the Old Testament because we're a New Testament church." Well, all right, let's go to the New Testament. In 1 Corinthians 10:6, Paul writes, "Now these things occurred as examples to

[them]." He's talking about the people in the Old Testament. By the way, you know what an example is, don't you? It's a pattern to follow. Paul says,

> Now these things occurred as examples, to keep us from setting our hearts on evil things as they did. Do not be idolaters, as some of them were; as it is written: "The people sat down to eat and drink and got up to indulge in pagan revelry." We should not commit sexual immorality, as some of them did—and in one day twenty-three thousand of them died. We should not test the Lord, as some of them did—and were killed by snakes. And do not grumble, as some of them did—and were killed by the destroying angel. These things happened to them as examples and were written down as warnings for us, on whom the fulfillment of the ages has come."

In other words you can't just set aside the Old Testament and say, "No, that doesn't have anything to do with me." The whole Bible is for us. And the whole Bible goes together. Sometimes well meaning people will say, "Tithing is an Old Testament concept, and since we're a New Testament church, we no longer have to tithe." All right, let's take that. For the sake of argument let's accept that as a fundamental premise. But I have to ask a question. Did you know there are over 500 prophecies in the Old Testament about the Second Coming of Christ? Can we discard those, too? Do we ignore those? Do we say that those 500 prophecies about the Second Coming of Christ are invalid now because we're New Testament Christians? That would be absurd.

The devil battles people more over baptism and tithing than anything else I know. Did you know that? You want to know why? Because those are starting points in our walk of obedience with Christ.

There are millions of people walking around the earth today, thinking they've been baptized when they really haven't. "What are you talking about?" You know, the ones who've been sprinkled or had a little bit poured on them, and think they've been baptized. There's not one half of one verse in the Bible that supports that. But they've been told by some denomination, misinformed theologian, church or preacher, that it's okay.

Unfortunately it's totally contrary to what the Word of God teaches. The Bible teaches that baptism has to picture the death, burial, and resurrection to be authentic, genuine baptism and only immersion pictures that. (See Romans 6:3-5.) Now follow this. If the devil can mess people up at baptism and keep them from obeying what God said they were to do and they live their whole life walking in disobedience, the devil's won. If he can somehow keep people from knowing what the Bible says they're to do, he's won and we lose.

Then comes the tithing issue. Tithing is elementary. It's a starting point for believers. It's not the ending point, it's the starting point. If the devil can hook you by getting you not to tithe and he can get you to disobey God in that area of your life, he can rob you of all the blessings God wants to give you. Once the devil gets you to disobey God in one area of your life, it's that much easier for him to get you to disobey God in other areas of your life as well.

Tithing is in the Old Testament. It really began with Cain and Abel. They were supposed to bring the "first fruits" to God. God evidently had told them, "The best of what you have belongs to Me, bring it to Me." Abel brought the first fruits, the best of what he had, but Cain didn't. God accepted Abel's offering but didn't accept Cain's, and Cain got mad. Do you realize the very first murder in all of human history was over an offering? (It's amazing to me people are still struggling over offerings and giving to God.)

Tithing continued with Abraham long before the Law. He

gave tithes to the High Priest Melchizedek in Genesis 14:17-24. Melchizedek was a pre-manifestation of the Lord Jesus Christ.

Remember Jacob's dream of the ladder at Bethel in Genesis 28? He spent the night dreaming of angels coming up and down a ladder and when he woke up in the morning he said, "God has been here." And he promised God, "If you'll bless me, I'll give you a tenth of everything I'll ever receive." This was long before the Law was ever given.

Tithing is also in the New Testament. One of the first passages is Matthew 23:23. I always laugh when someone says they don't think tithing is in the New Testament. Here it is! And guess Who's talking about it? Jesus! Read what He says, "Woe to you, teachers of the law and Pharisees, you hypocrites! You give a tenth [that's a tithe] of your spices—mint, dill and cumin." By the way, those are the three smallest spices known to man. "But you have neglected the more important matters of the law—justice, mercy and faithfulness." What these Pharisees were doing was tithing, even down to the very tiniest spices they had. But they were rude and unjust to people, did not practice mercy, and were not faithful to God. Now watch what Jesus says, "You should have practiced the latter, without neglecting the former." In other words, you should have practiced justice and mercy and faithfulness, but don't neglect your tithing.

It's a whole package. Just because you live a holy life is no excuse not to tithe. And just because you tithe, it's no excuse not to live a holy life. You have to do both. Jesus didn't abolish anything with regard to the Law and the Prophets. In Matthew 5:17-20 He says, "I have not come to abolish any of the Law or the Prophets. I've come to fulfill them" (paraphrase). Do you know what that means? It means He simply came to raise them to a *higher* standard.

Let me show you a contrast between the Old Testament

and the New Testament. In the Old Testament they had animal sacrifices. You say, "We don't have that in the New Testament anymore." You're right. We have something better. We have "living sacrifices" (Romans 12:1-2). There are still sacrifices; they're just not dead animals anymore.

In the Old Testament God established the tabernacle and the temple. In the New Testament He established the church. In the Old Testament God said, "Thou shalt not commit adultery." In the New Testament Jesus says, "I tell you that anyone who looks at a woman lustfully has already committed adultery with her in his heart" (Matthew 5:28). For more examples, in the Old Testament they had the Sabbath. In the New Testament we have the first day of the week. In the Old Testament they had the Law and the Prophets. In the New Testament we have the whole Bible and the Holy Spirit. They're not in conflict with each other; they complement each other. The New Testament is the fulfillment, the completion of the Old.

Do you see how Jesus raised things to a higher standard? He didn't abolish anything. He raised them to higher standards.

We've already seen the first two steps on the road to financial success.

First is to acknowledge the sovereignty of God—Attitude.

Second is to be aware of and avoid the subtlety of debt—Bondage.

In this chapter we discover step number three: **Adopt the centrality of the tithe.**

If we plan to get out of debt and get rid of our financial problems, the tithe has to be the absolute center of our plan. I'll tell you right up front, the pagan's portfolio does not include tithing, but the Christian's does. The single greatest thing you can do to turn your finances around is to make the choice to start trusting God and start tithing. It will change your life!

EIGHT PRINCIPLES OF TITHING

1. The tithe belongs to the Lord, not us.

Leviticus 27:30 says, "A tithe of everything . . . belongs to the LORD." In Malachi 3:10 God says, "Bring the tithe to Me, to My storehouse." If you study Joshua 7, the story of Achan, you'll find what Achan found out the hard way. You don't mess with the stuff that belongs to God. Study the story of the battle of Jericho. That was the first city they were to conquer in the Promised Land. All the spoils, the first fruits, the tithe, were set apart for the *Lord*. Achan took those spoils for himself. He thought, "God won't miss it; there's so much of it, and I can use this any way I want to." He paid a horrible price for his poor choice. Unfortunately so did his dear wife, his children, every family member he had, and even his animals. He found out the tithe belongs to the *Lord*.

2. We are to bring the whole tithe into the storehouse.

Malachi 3:10 says we are to *bring* it. The storehouse in the Old Testament was the temple. In the New Testament it's the local church. In Mark 12:41-44 Jesus is with His disciples, and the Bible says they "sat down opposite the place where the offerings were put." You know where that was? The temple. Jesus and the disciples went there and sat down, and evidently no one was fired up about it. It was a very common thing. Everybody knew you were giving.

Today people get nervous and superspiritual when it comes to giving. They'll tell you giving is a private matter between them and God and no one should know anything about it.

Anyway, when Jesus saw a widow who came and gave her offering, He said, "All these others gave out of their abundance but she gave sacrificially, she gave of all she had" (paraphrase).

Don't miss this. God wants us to *bring* our tithe to church. I noticed something when I was studying this one time. God doesn't want us mailing our tithe to the church or sending it with someone else. Of course, if you have to be out of town because you have to work or you're on vacation, that's a different story. But if you're not working or out of town on vacation, when the Lord's Day comes, God wants us to *bring* our tithe. Why? Because that's one way God can be sure we'll be in His house. And guess what? There are a lot of other things He wants to teach us from His Word. So by our *bringing* His tithe every week on the first day of the week, God can teach us all the things He wants us to know. "*Bring* the tithe to the storehouse."

By the way, remember we're to bring the tithe into the storehouse where we are cared for and fed. You don't eat at Burger King and say, "I appreciate the food, but I'm going to go down to Taco Bell and give them my money." It doesn't work that way. We're to *bring* the tithe, God's tithe, to the storehouse where we're fed and cared for.

3. We're to bring the whole tithe.

In Malachi 3:10 God said, "Bring the *whole* tithe, all ten percent." Sometimes we make excuses for people and say, "Start with two percent and work your way up." God doesn't tell anybody that. God doesn't say, "Work on it." God doesn't say, "Pray about it." God doesn't say, "See if somehow you can fit that into your budget." That's a lie of the devil. No. God clearly says, "Bring the *whole* tithe."

By the way, partial obedience won't bring partial blessings. Some people think, "I'll just obey God a little bit and that will bring me a little bit of blessings." Sorry. I've got some bad news for you. Partial obedience is total disobedience. I've said this before to the ladies in our church, if your husband goes on a trip and comes home and says, "I was ninety-nine percent faithful to you while I was gone," that's one hundred percent unfaithfulness. Isn't it? You bet it is. Here's some more bad news. Delayed obedience is disobedience. James 4:17 says, "Anyone, then, who knows the good he ought to do and doesn't do it, sins." So we're to bring the *whole* tithe.

4. We're to bring the whole tithe into the storehouse.

Again, in Malachi 3:10 notice God says to bring the whole tithe into the *storehouse*, not your house. Did you see that? That's a new revelation for some folks. It doesn't say take God's tithe and use it wherever you need it at your house. John Hagee, Pastor of the Cornerstone Church in San Antonio, has a message on tithing in which he says, "Some of you drove to church today in stolen cars. Some of you are sitting here in the service in stolen clothes. Some of you are living in houses that were built with stolen money. You took God's tithe and used it for yourself."[1] Now I may never be so bold as to say that, but I happen to think he's right. We're not to use God's tithe for our house. It's to be brought to *His house* and used for His purposes. It's His tithe.

5. We are to bring the whole tithe into the storehouse on Sunday, the first day of the week.

"Where do you get that?" First Corinthians 16:1-2 where the Apostle Paul told the Corinthian church, "Now about the collection for God's people: . . . On the first day of every week, each one of you should set aside a sum of money in keeping with his income, saving it up, so that when I come no collections will have to be made." The context is a "missionary offering." Paul's wanting them, when they come together for worship, in addition to the tithes and offerings they receive, to give something in accordance with their income and hold that for this mission offering so when he comes they don't have to take one. Our church does that. For several years we've been developing mission endowment funds. We're trying to save money in keeping with our income, so that when people come to us in need, mission needs, we won't have to take special offerings. That's very Biblical, and it's to be done on the first day of the week, *Sunday*.

By the way, we ought to be prepared to give ahead of time. It's Biblical to be prepared to give ahead of time. When you wait until the worship service to write your check for the offering, you're saying to those around you and to our great God above you, "I didn't plan to do this ahead of time." Someone will say, "Well, that's the way I've always done it." Then change the way you do things and do it at home. Plan to do it. Make that a part of your regular routine. Decide ahead of time to obey God.

6. The tithe belongs to God. We are not free to designate it, divide it, or direct it wherever we want.

The tithe is not yours, the tithe is not mine. It's *God's*! We can't designate it, divide it, or direct it wherever we want it to go. You'd be surprised how many different requests we get in our church. People say, "I want you to take my tithe and use it for this or apply it to that." We can't do that. That's *God's* tithe.

Now it's very Biblical to direct an offering above your tithe. It's interesting how sometimes people will say, "Wow, I can't believe how much money I've given to *God*." I want to say to them, "Go back and figure out what *God's* tithe is, and you'll probably discover you really didn't give that much to *God*." You see, the tithe already belongs to Him. We're not giving it to Him, we're giving it back to Him. That's why David said, "[Lord,] who am I, and who are my people, that we should be able to give as generously as this? Everything comes from you, and we have given you only what comes from your hand" (1 Chronicles 29:14). The tithe belongs to *God*.

7. In the Old Testament, priests administered the tithes and offerings. Today church leaders are in charge of that responsibility.

First Timothy 5:17 says, "The elders who *direct the affairs of the church* well are worthy of double honor"(emphasis added). That's their job. They are to take the tithes we bring, *God's* tithes and our offerings, and they are to use them and we're to trust them.

8. It's Biblical for leaders to set aside a sum of money from the tithes and offerings from God's people for mission work.

We already saw that in 1 Corinthians 16 and even Philippians 4. We've been doing that in our church for years. Besides the fact that we regularly support a large number of missionaries, we also have developed five separate mission endowment funds. Funds where we deposit $200,000 and let them earn interest. (Yes, that's over a million dollars in mission endowments.)

Here are our five mission endowment funds:

1. **The Founder's Fund.** (In honor of the people who started our church.) This fund exists to provide scholarships for people from our church who want to go to Bible college or Seminary.
2. **The Antioch Fund.** This fund exists to provide financial assistance for people to go on short-term mission trips.
3. **The Philippian Fund.** This fund exists to provide financial assistance for people to go on long-term mission trips.
4. **The Good Samaritan Fund.** This fund exists to provide financial assistance for people who need benevolent help.
5. **The Jerusalem Fund.** This fund exists to provide financial assistance to start new churches.

Because these funds have been designated to have over a million dollars in them, we will never have to touch the principal and can use the interest ("Somebody Else's" money) to fund mission needs from our church until Jesus returns.

Let me share a final thought. Some people have been conditioned to think financial problems are a way of life. That's simply not true. Here's what happens for too many people. Perhaps it's happened to you. When something good happens, you get a raise or a promotion or some unexpected money comes your way, you start thinking, "Oh, this is too good to be true. It won't last. Something bad is coming." Has that ever happened to you?

Here's a verse I hope will become a new life-verse for you. Proverbs 10:22: "The blessing of the LORD brings wealth, and he adds no trouble to it."

How can we get ourselves in a position where God will bless us with wealth and add no trouble to it? Second Chronicles 26:5 says of Uzziah that "as long as he sought the LORD, God gave him success." What's true of Uzziah will be true of you and true of me. As long as we seek the Lord, as long as we put Him first, God will bless us. The choice is ours.

How do we do that? If we're serious about getting out of debt and getting rid of financial problems, we need to make tithing the centerpiece of our financial planning.

Get this in your head and in your heart. God is the One behind our financial problems. And God is also the One behind our financial blessings. Once again, here's the promise. If we will bring the whole tithe into the storehouse, God will open the floodgates of heaven and throw out so much blessing that we will not have room enough to receive it (Malachi 3:8-10). Can you think of a better deal than that? I didn't think so.

Remember, we're the ones who determine whether God is behind the burdens or the blessings, the problems or the prosperity. The choice is ours.

. . . from the G.O.O.D. file

(simple ideas to encourage you to Get Out Of Debt)

Summertime can be a great time to make progress toward your goal of getting out of debt or, if you're not careful, it can be a dangerous time of getting into even more debt. The choice is yours.

The biggest culprit for getting further in debt during the summer months is vacations. Many people will use a credit card to charge plane flights, hotel accommodations, new clothes, meals, and even entertainment expenses with rationalizations like these: "We deserve this . . . we needed a break . . . we just had to get away . . .", etc. The problem is, you can stack up a small mountain of debt with a one or two-week vacation where you charge everything. The truth is, you'll be paying for your vacation for many months after the memories are long gone and, more often than not, paying with interest, too! (Ouch!)

Action Plans

Here are some suggestions to help you get OUT of debt rather than getting INTO more debt during the summer months:

1. Don't charge anything this summer. Make it a rule you absolutely won't break.

2. Don't buy new clothes just for the summer. Get one more summer out of the ones you have.

3. Have some backyard barbecues instead of going out to eat. (You'll save a lot of money here and won't ever have to stand in line.)

4. Use coupons for your weekly grocery shopping. You can save a lot with coupons.

5. Make a concerted effort to conserve on electricity and water during the summer months. (You don't have to have it like an icebox inside or all green outside. Once-a-week watering is plenty.)

6. Cut back on long-distance phone calls and only make calls you have to make during the off hours. (Evenings and weekends.)

7. Have a garage sale. (You'll end up with a cleaner garage and some extra money for your family.)

8. Encourage every member of your family to live within his/her means. In other words, always spend less than you earn, and put something in savings each week.

Not only will these things help you have a better summer, they'll also help you **Get Out Of Debt!**

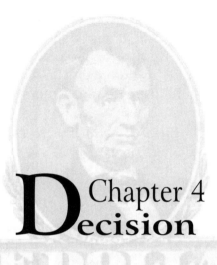

D Chapter 4
ecision

"You don't make decisions because they are easy;
you don't make them because they are cheap;
you don't make them because they're popular;
you make them because they are RIGHT."
—Theodore Hesburgh

Solomon wrote in Proverbs 13:7, "One man pretends to be rich, yet has nothing; another pretends to be poor, yet has great wealth." There's a verse that describes people in America. In their best selling book, *The Millionaire Next Door*, Thomas Stanley and William Danko shared several shocking revelations. They said that most millionaires buy their suits off the rack. Most millionaires purchase and drive used cars. Most millionaires shop at Sears. Most millionaires make their kids earn their money rather than just giving it to them. And most millionaires always live well below their means. That's why they're millionaires. Unfortunately the majority of people in America are not millionaires. And if they continue their current spending habits, they never will be.

Not long ago *The Fort Worth Star Telegram* ran a series of articles on money and finances. Here's a quote from one of those:

> With the economy booming Americans have been on a buying binge and they've got the bulging credit card balances to prove it. Consumer debt, or debt other than mortgages, rose to $1.344 trillion in 1998 from $1.096 trillion in 1995. According to the Federal Reserve, the average American household carries a $2,800 balance each month on credit cards. But many are much more than that. Last year more than 24,000 people visited the Consumer Credit Counseling Service of Greater Fort Worth and west Texas' 28 offices to get help managing their debt. The typical client in our area owed $23,703 on ten credit cards.
>
> "The people I see didn't realize how much they were spending," says Kay Warden, a debt counselor at CCCS's office in Burleson. "They filled out credit card applications at Foley's and other stores without adding it up and if I asked them how much they spent on Christmas, they had no idea."[1]

Obviously financial problems can be incredibly complex. However getting out of a money mess is merely a matter of following some simple steps. So far we've seen the first three steps to achieve financial success:

First, we need to acknowledge the sovereignty of God—Attitude.

Second, we need to be aware of and avoid the subtlety of debt—Bondage.

Third, we need to adopt the centrality of the tithe—Choice.

In this chapter I want to examine the fourth step on the road to financial success: **we need to accept God's plan and enjoy the security of obedience—Decision**.

I want to share a story with you from 2 Kings 5:1-15. Even though it's in the Old Testament and even though it's not about finances or money, there's some great wisdom we can apply to every area of our lives, especially our finances.

NAAMAN THE LEPER

The story begins in 2 Kings 5:1,"Now Naaman was commander of the army of the king of Aram. He was a great man in the sight of his master and highly regarded, because through him the LORD had given victory to Aram. He was a valiant soldier, [watch these next four words] but he had leprosy."

Remember, the most insidious disease the human body can ever contract is leprosy because you lose all of your pain sensors. Verses 2-15:

> Now bands from Aram had gone out and had taken captive a young girl from Israel, and she served Naaman's wife. She said to her mistress, "If only my master would see the prophet who is in Samaria! He would cure him of his leprosy."
> Naaman went to his master and told him what the girl from Israel had said. "By all means, go," the king of Aram replied. "I will send a letter to the king of Israel." So Naaman left, taking with him ten talents of silver, six thousand shekels of gold and ten sets of clothing. The letter that he took to the king of Israel read: "With this letter I am sending my servant Naaman to you so that you may cure him of his leprosy."
> As soon as the king of Israel read the letter, he tore his robes and said, "Am I God? Can I kill and bring back to life? Why does this fellow send someone to me to be cured of his leprosy? See how he is trying to pick a quarrel with me!"

When Elisha the man of God heard that the king of Israel had torn his robes, he sent him this message: "Why have you torn your robes? Have the man come to me and he will know that there is a prophet in Israel." So Naaman went with his horses and chariots and stopped at the door of Elisha's house. Elisha sent a messenger to say to him, "Go, wash yourself seven times in the Jordan, and your flesh will be restored and you will be cleansed."

But Naaman went away angry and said, "I thought that he would surely come out to me and stand and call on the name of the LORD his God, wave his hand over the spot and cure me of my leprosy. Are not Abana and Pharpar, the rivers of Damascus, better than any of the waters of Israel? Couldn't I wash in them and be cleansed?" So he turned and went off in a rage.

Naaman's servants went to him and said, "My father, if the prophet had told you to do some great thing, would you not have done it? How much more, then, when he tells you, 'Wash and be cleansed'!" So he went down and dipped himself in the Jordan seven times, as the man of God had told him, and his flesh was restored and became clean like that of a young boy.

Then Naaman and all his attendants went back to the man of God. He stood before him and said, "Now I know that there is no God in all the world except in Israel. Please accept now a gift from you servant."

Now Naaman was the commander of the king of Aram (Syria). He was highly respected and a valiant soldier, but he had leprosy. From his life and situation there are at least six life-changing lessons we can learn that have direct application to our finances.

Six Life-changing Lessons
Lesson #1: No one is immune from problems.

It doesn't matter whether you are the commander of an army or the CEO of a corporation or the staff member of a major church. No one's immune from problems. Naaman had leprosy. What's your problem?

Lesson #2: God will use the most unlikely sources to get us what we need.

In Naaman's situation it was a servant girl that God used to lead him to the cure of his problems.

Lesson #3: The answer to our problems won't usually be what we want to hear.

Isn't that interesting? It won't usually be what we *want* to hear. Elisha told Naaman, "Go down and dip yourself seven times in the Jordan River."

Lesson #4: We'll be tempted to come up with our own plan.

Too often God tells us to do something in a certain way and we'll say, "Yeah, okay, but I'm going to try it this way." Or we'll try to modify what He tells us. Naaman got angry at what he'd been told and came up with his own plan. He said, "The rivers Abana and Pharpar are far nicer than any of the rivers of Israel." Ever know someone like that?

Lesson #5: Wise friends will always encourage us to do what God says.

One of the surest ways you can tell true friends is: they will always tell you what you need to hear, not what you want to hear. Naaman's friends went to him and his servants went to him, and they encouraged him to do what the prophet told him to do.

Lesson #6: God's way is always the right way.

Naaman eventually did what he was told and was healed. There is great security in obedience. You're never going to obey God and regret it. I've never been around anyone, at the end of their life after following God and being faithful to God, who says, "I sure wish I hadn't been a goody-two-shoes. I wish I hadn't done all the right things. I wish I hadn't lived a holy life. I wish I hadn't done everything I could for God." You know what I have heard, though, hundreds and hundreds of times? "If I could do it all over again, I'd sure do things a whole lot differently. I would have lived for God. I wish I would have followed God's plan."

Let me tell you something about obedience. Obedience always requires two things and there's no exception to this.

Number one is faith. Obedience to God will always require faith on our part. Faith literally means, "Can I trust God to do this? Do I have the faith to trust God? This sounds unbelievable. I don't know how this would ever work. God's calling me to do something but can I trust God to do this?" It takes faith. The issue is: am I willing to trust God and do it His way?

Number two is faithfulness. Obedience requires our faithfulness. You have to ask, "Can God trust me to do this?" In other words, am I willing to hang in there and see this through to the end?

We're all real good at starting out doing the right stuff. Every January millions of people go through their annual ritual of making New Year's resolutions and all kinds of new commitments. It's a time when we all want to start out right. But so many times we don't even get to the middle of February and we've already blown the commitments we made at the beginning of the year. It takes faithfulness—will you and I hang in there and see this through to the end?

BE PREPARED

When you decide to get out of debt and get your finances in order at least three things will happen:

1. When you make the decision to follow God's plan, you are going to get discouraged.

You need to know up front you're going to get discouraged. You're going to see other people buying new cars, buying new clothes, and putting additions on their homes. Your neighbors are going to come back from Cancun after a week of vacation and those kinds of things will discourage you. You'll be tempted to say, "Why am I doing all this? Why am I disciplining myself? Why am I going without so I can try to get out of debt when they look like they're really happy?" Be prepared ahead of time. There are going to be some discouragements coming your way.

2. You're going to get distracted.

There are going to be some things that come along and you're going to find yourself rationalizing, "We have to get the car fixed and the kids want to go on their school trip and we all need new shoes," etc. The distractions will come, and if you don't watch it, your rationalizations can be pretty convincing and you'll get clear off track and the devil will get you right back in that same bondage again.

3. There will be detractors.

There will always be people who make fun of you. My biggest attacks have come from family members. (Not my immediate family. I tell them they can move out if they don't like the way we're doing things.) But I can't control those extended family members who always have "a better way of running your life than you do." Sometimes it's your friends; sometimes it's the people you work with. They'll say things to you and their arguments can sure sound good. Before you know it, you can almost convince yourself they're right and you must be wrong. Be prepared for that ahead of time so you can stay on target with your goal of getting out of debt and being free from financial stress.

CALLED TO THE RIGHT WAY

Back in October, 1999, our church had some tremendous financial needs such as getting out of debt and building facilities. So we'd prayed as a leadership about what we should do. We had a number of capital stewardship companies contact us. Big finance consulting firms contacted us for the better part of three years, saying, "We can help your church. What you need to do is have a capital stewardship campaign and get your people to commit the money you need." I'll admit, I've always felt uncomfortable with capital stewardship campaigns. But we went ahead anyway and thought, "We're going to be out of debt and probably should go ahead and do this."

We went ahead and signed a contract with a professional fund-raising company. The guy came and met with us and in the first meeting there was an obvious uneasiness in the meeting. I couldn't explain it, but I knew something wasn't right. Following that meeting several of the people who'd been present asked me, independently of the others, why we were using a professional fund-raising company in the first place. A couple of them said, "You ought to do our campaign. You're telling the guy what we ought to do. Why do we have him here?"

So I thought, "Maybe I need to back off and not say anything in the next meeting." The next meeting came, and this time those in the meeting were much more resolute in their objections. They said, "We don't think we ought to be doing this." As I listened to those involved in the meetings, I had a disturbing thought. "Is this the servant girl of Naaman here? Am I wanting to do things my way when God has another way He wants us to go? Do I need to listen to these people because God wants us to do it a whole different way?" I decided to fast and pray, and as I did, God made it very clear to me, "You need to help get the people in the church out of debt first. Then you'll have all the money you'll ever need for all the things I will tell you to do."

So I went to my office and got all the books I had in my library on finances and debt and I got a book by Larry Burkett called *Debt-Free Living*. When I opened it, I noticed the date at the top of the book. (When I read a book I always write the date I begin to read it in the top right-hand corner). I had written "7/31/89." Suddenly I remembered what was going on back in 1989. I was pastoring a church in Florida. We were showing a series of videos by Larry Burkett. Every night we showed them, the place was packed. People were interested in getting out of debt and learning how to get out of their financial messes. Everybody I knew was in there. Young couples, older folks, it was wall-to-wall people.

We were watching these videos on how to get out of debt. As a result of that series, Janis and I made some serious commitments. We got rid of cable TV, we stopped the newspaper, we stopped going out to eat, we started eating sandwiches for lunch, and things were going great. At the time we were miserably in debt, but thanks to applying God's principles, we paid off both our cars and every credit card we had. It was a miracle that God was getting us out of debt. We were making extra principal payments on our house and were in the process of paying it off. It was a great time in our lives. I even told some friends, "I lived like a king back in the '80s."

After looking at that book in my office, remembering what it was like back in 1989, I went home and asked my wife for all our current bills. (Remember now, it's October of 1999— ten years later.) I got my calculator out and began to add it up. As I added it up, I realized that now, ten years later, we were twice as much in debt as we were back in 1989. In ten years we were in much worse financial shape than we had been back in 1989. Unfortunately, although it looked as if we'd made progress and were actually doing much better, the truth was, we were doing much worse.

As I sat there and considered that in the next two years I would have two of my children in college, I uttered something intensely spiritual, "This is nuts!" And (are you ready for this?) it hit me. Having all the best books on money and finances won't help me. Having all the right principles and all the best tape series and getting excited about the messages, none of that's going to do it. We have to make a decision and we have to make a decision now!

I made a fresh commitment before God. "I'm going to apply these principles, and I'm going to get back to doing the right things in our finances and I'm going to stick with it no matter what."

I got my family together for what we affectionately call a "come to Jesus" meeting, and I said, "Guess what, ladies and gentlemen, and children. We're getting out of debt! And there's going to be some changes around here." We had a whole series of "come to Jesus" meetings with our family, many of them impromptu, many at a much higher decibel level than normal. And my family finally got it. They realized how serious I was about this and that I wasn't backing down. So our family made the commitment to get debt free!

When I went back to my office, I put that book by Larry Burkett (with the 1989 date written in it) on top of my computer because I wanted to have a daily reminder that I would never again go backwards financially. I was going to get out of debt. The principles do work. But I have to put them to work in my life. It's just like Jesus said, "You will know the truth, and the truth will set you free" (John 8:32). It's not the truth that sets you free, it's when you know it that it sets you free. We all have Bibles, but just setting them on the coffee table is not enough. We have to apply what's in the Bible to our lives. We have to make the decision we're going to do it.

How did we get off track from where we were in 1989?

Easy. We got discouraged, got distracted, and listened to the detractors. To be honest, when I saw that date in Burkett's book, I was tempted to stop writing the dates in the front of books when I read them. That's one way to deal with it, but that's like the warning light on the dashboard again. We can disable the light to keep it from blinking, or we can heed the warning and deal with the problem.

God never calls us to the easy way or the lazy way or the inexpensive way or the convenient way. He always calls us to the right way. Our job is to decide to listen. Our responsibility is to obey Him and do what He tells us. When we obey, there is great security in that. When we apply God's principles, God's way, we'll always get God's results.

SEVEN SIMPLE STRATEGIES TO GET OUT OF DEBT

Here are some simple strategies to help you get out of debt and be free forever from financial stress and difficulty.

1. Trust God.

Matthew 6:33 says, "But seek first his kingdom and his righteousness, and all these things will be given to you as well."

2. Tithe.

Without question that's the master key to financial success. Every Christian ought to be a faithful, consistent tither. I'll tell you why we haven't been in worse shape than we've been financially. We have always been faithful tithers. Even since I was a kid, I've been a faithful tither. But tithing alone is not going to do it. You've got to control your spending and do the other things God says as well.

I want to extend a challenge to every business owner who reads this book. Every Christian ought to be a tither and every business owner ought to be tithing his personal income. But let me challenge you to go "the second mile" as a business owner. I challenge you to tithe your business income as well. You may ask, "Why should I do that?" Because I've seen what it has done to our own church since we made that decision.

Every leader in our church, every elder, every deacon, every Sunday school teacher, every member of our staff are tithers. But you know what? We also tithe what's given in the offerings on Sundays to our church. Since we've done that, which has been several years ago now, God has phenomenally blessed our church. The same blessing that's available to us personally is available corporately to a body. In fact, I won't support any parachurch organization or any ministry that does not tithe. Why? Because if an individual can be under a curse for not tithing, a ministry can be under a curse as well (Malachi 3:9).

I want to challenge you to consider that. The same blessings you enjoy personally from tithing can be yours corporately as you tithe from your business income. Think what would happen in our churches if every businessperson in America started tithing their business income this week? Will you lead the way?

3. Develop a Budget.

Luke 14:28-29 says, "Suppose one of you wants to build a tower. Will he not first sit down and estimate the cost to see if he has enough money to complete it?" Do you understand what Jesus was saying? "Won't this tower builder put together a budget? Won't he put together a written plan?" Luke continues, "For if he lays the foundation and is not able to finish it, everyone who sees it will ridicule him, saying, 'This fellow began to build and was not able to finish.'" Jesus encouraged planning, preparing, and strategizing.

a. **You need to develop a "G.O.O.D File."** What's a "G.O.O.D. File?" G-O-O-D stands for: **Get Out Of Debt.** Every time I hear the word "good" or anytime I hear someone say something's good, I'm just reminded, Get Out Of Debt. That's the reminder I need to get out of debt. Develop a "G.O.O.D. File."

b. **Both husband and wife need to see the whole picture on a regular basis**. If you'll look at your debt and your bills on a regular basis, it will seriously curtail your spending. Trust me. Too often the wife handles the bills or the husband pays the bills and the other mate doesn't see it. So they keep spending, getting further and further in debt, and the wife who's struggling to pay everything or the husband who's struggling to pay everything doesn't want to hurt the other one's feelings and say, "No, we really can't afford that." So you get deeper and deeper in debt and it's because you didn't take an honest look at your financial situation on a weekly basis.

c. **I would recommend that you read and listen to everything you can on getting out of debt.** I'm always encouraged by the people in our church who are already out of debt who always look forward to the next sermon series on finances or the newest book on effective money management. Someone might ask, "If you're already out of debt, why would you want to hear and read things about getting out of debt?" I think the answer is simple: So you stay out of debt.

4. Get Out Of Debt.

Proverbs 22:7 says, "The rich rule over the poor, and the borrower is servant to the lender." Get out of debt. Stop being a servant to some financial institution. Get out of debt and just be God's servant.

a. **Remember the word INTEREST.** Don't forget what that word really means. If I'm paying interest, "SOMEONE ELSE" is making money; I'm not.

b. **Remember what the letters for DEBT stand for. D-E-B-T:** Dumb Explanation for Buying Things. Remember that. If you have to use debt to buy something, just use those letters, D-E-B-T. It will help encourage you. Or Don't Even Buy That if you have to go into debt to get it.

c. **Don't buy anything you can't pay cash for.** If you can't pay cash for it, just wait. We don't like to delay our own gratification. We like to have what we want when we want it—right now. But, friend, you'll either pay now and play later or you'll play now and pay later. If you play now and pay later, you'll pay interest and SOMEONE ELSE will get rich, not you.

d. **Start paying off your debts one at a time.** Start paying them off. It takes discipline to do that. By the way, getting out of debt includes paying off our homes. I've heard people say, "I'm out of debt," and I'll ask, "Is your home paid off, too?" And they'll say, "No. We haven't paid off our home." Then you're not really out of debt. Larry Burkett says, "I advise you to accelerate your mortgage payments to retire the debt as rapidly as possible. I believe one of the essential foundation blocks of a Biblically oriented financial plan is a debt-free home. This should be the goal of all Christians."[2] Get out of debt.

5. *Start saving.*

Proverbs 13:11 says, "Dishonest money dwindles away, but he who gathers money little by little makes it grow."

a. **Always spend less than you earn.** If you'll always spend less than what you get paid every week, you're going to get out of debt and you're going to get financial freedom in your life.

b. **Set a goal to have money left over before your next payday.** I get an allowance every week. (Sounds elementary, doesn't it?) My wife gets an allowance every week. My children get an allowance every week. You know what my goal is and the goal I try to teach every member of my family? The goal is to try to get to the next payday with money in your pocket. Then you're ahead of the game. If you keep doing it on a regular basis, you can save up a sizable amount of money and be able to do some nice things with it. For instance, one year I bought Christmas gifts for everyone on my list with cash that I'd saved up by not spending everything I had every week. My goal is to try to end every week with some extra money in my pocket. It's not that hard, and the benefits are wonderful.

c. **After you give God's tithe, try to save 10% for yourself.** Pay yourself just like a bill and put it in savings. This will add up fast.

6. *Begin an emergency fund.*

Proverbs 6:6-11 talks about the ant and how he stores up things in the summer and Solomon says, "Sluggard, go check out the ant and see how he does it." The Bible is clear we need to be prepared for emergencies.

a. **Plan for rainy days because somewhere down the road it's going to rain.**

b. **Don't use your emergency fund to go out to dinner or go on vacation.** Those are not emergencies; those are indulgences. Have a fund just for emergencies.

c. **You need to have a will.** Find a Christian attorney or a Christian financial planner. Contact them and tell them, "I need to have a will." Don't be one of those who says, "I don't have that much. What do I need a will for?" You need to have a will. One of the best investments you'll ever make is to have a will so you can take care of your family and take care of your children. By the way, I recommend (we've done this in our own will) you tithe 10% of all your assets back to your local church. Why? Because when we're no longer here on this earth, we want God to bless the administration of our assets. This gives us the opportunity, even in our death, to once again acknowledge His sovereign Lordship in our lives and maybe we'd like to have one more opportunity to say, "Thank you, God, for all the financial blessings You've given to our family."

7. Don't quit or turn back.

Don't get sidetracked by what anybody says. Don't allow yourself to be distracted by what happens and don't quit or turn back. In Luke 9:62 Jesus says, "No one who puts his hand to the plow and looks back is fit for service in the kingdom of God." Remember Naaman. The issue wasn't the dipping, it was the obeying. He obeyed God and God blessed him.

My dream for our church and for churches all across America is twofold. The first is this: To help get every Christian out of debt. The second is: to raise up a generation of people who will be lifetime tithers. Because if I can teach you how to tithe and get you committed to tithing, I can get you "under the spout where the blessings come out," and God will bless you no matter what happens in the days ahead.

. . . from the G.O.O.D. file

(simple ideas to encourage you to Get Out Of Debt)

Here are some practical tips that will help you enjoy the Christmas holidays and not look back with regret once January gets here.

1. Don't let shopping take priority over worship. If we do, we miss the whole point of Christmas.

2. Don't get caught up trying to outbuy or outdo anybody else when you do your Christmas shopping.

3. Don't charge the gifts you buy for others. Yes, you probably won't buy as much, but you won't cry much either later on when the bills come due.

4. Give practical, usable gifts that will help meet needs instead of wasting money on frivolous gifts that will go back in the box, in the closet, the attic, or the next garage sale once the holidays are over.

5. Make sure the Lord is at the top of your Christmas list. (After all, it's His birthday we celebrate.) Giving at your church's Christmas Eve services provides an excellent way to teach your children and model for your family what Christmas is all about.

6. Do take the time to bake Christmas cookies, go see Christmas lights, watch a Christmas video, or some other activity that will help draw your family closer together.

7. Stay on target with your goal to become debt free. Don't allow your emotions and the *spirit of giving* to cause you to get off track and spend what you don't have on things you don't need or have to give.

8. Do take time to thank God for all your blessings and to reflect over the year.

9. Remember the best gift you can give, especially to your own family, is YOU.

Action Plan

Get free from the bondage of financial stress and debt. During the holidays stop by a Christian bookstore and check out the number of excellent resources available on managing your money, practicing Biblical stewardship, and getting out of debt. They'll make great Christmas gifts for your family and friends.

Chapter 5
Encouragement

"Here's the bottom line: God says,
'You give Me everything and I'll take care of you.
Or you keep it all and take care of yourself.'"
—John Maxwell

One of the tragic ironies of life is that money and things can never satisfy us. Yet many people are chasing after them with breakneck speed. On the other hand God can satisfy us and take care of everything we need. Yet many people still don't believe it.

Perhaps the following will encourage you.

FIVE CRUCIAL QUESTIONS
ANSWERED BY SCRIPTURE

1. Where do all the resources in the world come from?

Psalm 24:1, "The earth is the LORD'S and everything in it, the world, and all who live in it."

2. How can I get those resources?

Deuteronomy 8:18, "Remember the LORD your God, for it is he who gives you the ability to produce wealth. . . ."

3. When can I get those resources?

Luke 6:38a, "Give, and it will be given to you. . . ."

4. Who decides how many of those resources I get?

Luke 6:38c, "For with the measure you use, it will be measured to you."

5. Can I ever be free from financial problems?

Proverbs 10:22, "The blessing of the LORD brings wealth, and he adds no trouble to it."

Billy Graham said, "If a person gets his attitude toward money straight, it will help him straighten out almost every other area of his life." Do you have the right attitude toward money? Are you trusting God? It has always amazed me how people are more than willing to trust God for their eternal salvation, but when it comes to their finances they start getting a little nervous. (What's wrong with that picture?)

Martin Luther said, "There are three conversions: the heart, the mind, and the purse." Until we learn to trust God with our money, we aren't really converted. Judging by the average giving of Christians in America (which is now less than 3% of our annual income according to the most recent surveys), there are a lot of unconverted people in our churches.

FIVE REASONS PEOPLE DON'T TRUST GOD WITH THEIR FINANCES

1. Ignorance

They don't know any better.

2. Disobedience

They do know better, but ignore what God says.

3. Selfishness

They don't care what God says and want to keep it all for themselves.

4. Worry

They're scared to trust God and walk by faith.

5. Immaturity

They haven't grown to the place in their relationship with God where they can trust Him to do what He says He will do.

Would you let a thief be president of a bank? Of course not. Then why do we let thieves and robbers lead the church? No one in their right mind would put money in a bank where it was a known fact the president was a thief. Yet churches will allow leaders to remain in positions of leadership who are not faithfully and regularly tithing their income back to God through the local church. Could this help explain, at least in part, the continual plague of financial problems and struggles among our churches?

God is pretty emphatic in Malachi 3 that we are robbing Him when we don't bring our tithe to the storehouse. If every Christian ought to be a tither, and they should (giving at least 10% of your weekly earnings to God), then certainly every leader in the church ought to be a tither as well. In fact, leaders ought to be tithers as a matter of public record.

Larry Burkett says,

The word tithe literally means a tenth. Since this is the minimum amount mentioned in the Bible, it would be logical to
assume that it's the minimum amount God wants from a
believer. It we can't return even the smallest part to God, it
merely testifies that the whole has never been surrendered to
Him. In the book of Malachi, the prophet confronted God's
people with the fact that they didn't love Him. Yet, they said
that they did love Him. But the evidence against them was that
they didn't give. This is the only place in Scripture where God
ever told His people to test Him. Plus this passage makes the
principle of tithing clear. It's an outside indicator of an inside
spiritual condition. It's our testimony that God owns everything in our lives.[1]

If you're not tithing, you ought to start this week as a
matter of obedience to God. Not to mention the other benefits that come with it. If you're a leader in a local church or a
parachurch organization, you ought to step down from your
position of leadership until you begin obeying God in this crit-
ical area of your life. Why? In Malachi 3 God says the whole
nation was "under a curse" because the people weren't tithing
(Malachi 3:9). Like Achan (in Joshua 7), who single-handedly
took the blessing off the nation of Israel, you, too, could be
placing your church or ministry in a position where God can't
bless it because of your disobedience.

Leaders ought to be tithers as a matter of record and as
an "example to the flock that is under their charge." Those
who refuse to tithe or to be held accountable for tithing ought
not be leaders in God's church or in any organization that rep-
resents God.

SEVEN LAWS OF PROSPERITY

You can't violate any of these laws and expect God to
bless you financially. Here they are:

1. The Law of Sowing and Reaping (2 Corinthians 9:6)

"Remember this: Whoever sows sparingly will also reap sparingly, and whoever sows generously will also reap generously." If you don't sow anything, you won't reap anything. You will reap what you sow. You will reap more than you sow, and you will reap later than you sow.

2. The Law of Blessing (Psalm 1:1-6)

Blessed is the man
   who does not walk in the counsel of the wicked
or stand in the way of sinners
   or sit in the seat of mockers.
But his delight is in the law of the Lord,
   and on his law he meditates day and night.
He is like a tree planted by streams of water,
   which yields its fruit in season
and whose leaf does not wither.
   Whatever he does prospers.

Not so the wicked!
   They are like chaff
   that the wind blows away.
Therefore the wicked will not stand in the judgment,
   nor sinners in the assembly of the righteous.

For the Lord watches over the way of the righteous,
   but the way of the wicked will perish.

Blessing always follows obedience. Don't ever forget that.

3. The Law of Origination (James 1:17)

"Every good and perfect gift is from above, coming down from the Father of the heavenly lights, who does not change like shifting shadows." Deuteronomy 8:18 says, "But remember the Lord your God, for it is he who gives you the ability to produce wealth, and so confirms his covenant. . . ." It all originates with God.

4. The Law of Generosity (2 Corinthians 9:10-11)

"Now he who supplies seed to the sower and bread for food will also supply and increase your store of seed and will enlarge the harvest of your righteousness. You will be made rich in every way so that you can be generous on every occasion, and through us your generosity will result in thanksgiving to God." God will always be generous to those who are generous to His work.

5. The Law of Determination (Luke 6:38)

"Give, and it will be given to you. A good measure, pressed down, shaken together and running over, will be poured into your lap. For with the measure you use, it will be measured to you." You and I determine the level of our blessings.

6. The Law of Firstfruits (Proverbs 3:9-10)

"Honor the Lord with your wealth, with the firstfruits of all your crops; then your barns will be filled to overflowing, and your vats will brim over with new wine." When we give God our best, our firstfruits, His blessings overflow in our lives.

7. The Law of Trust (Malachi 3:8-10)

"Will a man rob God? Yet you rob me. But you ask, 'How do we rob you?' In tithes and offerings. You are under a curse—the whole nation of you—because you are robbing me. Bring the whole tithe into the storehouse, that there may be food in my house. Test me in this," says the Lord Almighty, "and see if I will not throw open the floodgates of heaven and pour out so much blessing that you will not have room enough for it." It's not a matter of accounting. It's a matter of attitude. Do we trust God?

Sir John Templeton, one of the world's most respected investors and investment counselors, said that countless people had asked him over the years, "What's the best investment?" He said he never hesitated to offer this surprising answer: tithing. Here is what Sir John wrote: "In all my fifty-two years before I retired as an investment counselor, we were helping people, literally hundreds of thousands of people, with their wealth. In all of those years there was only one investment which never proved faulty, and that was tithing—giving at least 10% of your income to your church. In all my history I have never seen a family who tithes for as long as ten years that didn't become both prosperous and happy. That is the best investment anyone can select."[2]

Jesus said in Matthew 6:21, "For where your treasure is, there your heart will be also." Do you and I really have a heart for God and the things of God? If we do, our giving will show it.

. . . from the G.O.O.D. file

(simple ideas to encourage you to Get Out Of Debt)

Implementing a Reward System

One of the best ways to get out of debt is to implement a reward system in your family. Let me share a personal example:

Years ago when we were living in Florida, I'd made the commitment to Janis that we would return to her family's home in Oklahoma every Christmas. (Be careful what you promise, guys.) Obviously it cost a great deal of money each year, especially as our young family was growing. Plane flights, rental cars, Christmas gifts. How did we do it? We charged it on a credit card. Every year. And then we'd spend the rest of the year paying it off.

We did that for several years until one year in the fall I made the announcement we weren't going to do that anymore. I shared with our family that it was nuts to keep charging our vacation, Christmas gifts, etc., on a credit card, and then spend the rest of the year trying to pay it off, plus interest! I announced we would be staying in Florida that Christmas, and if we were able to save up the money to go next year, we'd go.

Well, guess what happened? One year later somehow (miraculously?) we were able to save more than enough money to fly back to Oklahoma from Florida, buy nicer than normal gifts, have some extra spending money on our trip, and even have some left over when we returned home. Oh, and by the way, we've never charged another vacation since.

Action Plan

Implement a reward system. Save up the funds needed ahead of time, and the reward is not only a debt-free vacation but also the reward of not having to pay interest. The reward system works not only for vacations but also for virtually anything else you could need or want. And it's a G.O.O.D. way to manage your resources.

Chapter 6
Funding

*"Stewardship is the use of God-given resources
for the accomplishment of God-given goals."*
—Ron Blue

WE ALREADY HAVE THE RESOURCES

Would you be shocked if I told you that God has already provided the funding to completely underwrite every ministry, minister, mission, missionary, and Christian enterprise in the world? Sound far-fetched? I'm not the first one to say it. Here's what Larry Burkett said, "Consider what would happen in America if Christians committed themselves to the Lord. Empty Tomb, Inc., notes that if American church members would increase their giving to an average of ten percent (current estimates are that Christians in America are giving less than 3%), there would be an extra $69 billion for overseas missions."[1] That's just for missions! It's been estimated there would also be an additional $150 billion in income for American churches if we could just get Christians to tithe.

Think of it. No special offerings. No special fund-raising drives. Just Christians simply and faithfully obeying God by bringing the tithe to the storehouse every Sunday here in America. It would result in an extra $219 billion dollars for the kingdom. It's currently estimated that there are 350,000 churches in America. That would mean an additional $625,714.29 for every church in America. Could your church use an extra $625,714.29? Absolutely. So how do we get to the place where that can happen? We have to teach our people God's supernatural system for funding His work here on the earth.

Not long ago I heard the story of Sam Houston, the famous renegade from Texas. I'm told this story is true. It seems that as Sam was about to be baptized in a river, the preacher said, "Sam, when I dunk you into the water, all of your sins are going to come out of you and into the water." As Sam Houston reflected on his life of drinking, carousing, womanizing and gambling, he bowed his head. The pastor asked, "Sam, what are you doing?" Sam replied, "I'm saying a prayer for the folks downstream."

Then the pastor said, "Sam, you better take your wallet out of your pocket or it will get soaking wet." To which Sam replied, "Nothin' doin'—if I'm going to be baptized, I want my wallet baptized, too!"

If we're ever going to reach our financial potential in our personal lives, our churches, our ministries, and in our ability to fund worldwide missions causes, we're going to have to have our wallets baptized, too! Dr. Homer G. Lindsay, former pastor of the famous First Baptist Church in Jacksonville, Florida, said, "I've found, in all my years of ministry, that if people don't get victory when it comes to tithing and giving offerings above the tithe, they don't get victory in the other areas of their lives as well."[2]

When I came to Arlington back in August of 1992, the church was averaging less than 200 in morning worship, offerings averaged just over $3,300 a week, and the total given to missions (for the year) was $14,366.31. The church also had a considerable amount of debt. Nine years later morning worship has already exceeded 2000, offerings average over $65,000 a week, we've given over one million dollars to missions and our entire church campus is completely debt free. When you add the 101 acres we've purchased to relocate our ministry, the total is worth in excess of 10 million dollars.

What made the difference? We've taught our people God's supernatural system for funding His work in our world: tithing. Is every member of our church a tither? Not yet. But we're headed in that direction. As you can see from the statistics, those who've already learned to trust God by tithing have helped make a phenomenal difference in the funds we have available for our ministry. And we haven't even discussed offerings (giving above the tithe) or what happens when our people get out of debt and our churches get out of debt. Talk about an exponential blessing upon the Body of Christ! There are no limits to what God could do through us if we'd just learn to trust Him in the area of tithing and managing our finances according to the principles of His Word.

Henry Crowell, the founder of Quaker Oats, was so moved by a sermon by Dwight L. Moody that he made a remarkable commitment to the Lord. He said, "Lord, I can't be a preacher, but I can be a good businessman. If you will make me money, I will use it in your services." He gave far beyond the tithe for over 40 years.

William Colgate ran away from home at age 17. He tithed the first dollar he made as an employee. Soon he was made partner of the company and ultimately owned Colgate Palmolive Company. His giving grew from 20% to 30% to 40%, and finally he was giving all of his income to the Lord.

R.G. LeTourneau, creator and manufacturer of giant, earth-moving machinery, by the end of his career reversed the percentages and gave God 90% while he lived on 10%. J.L. Kraft of the Kraft Cheese Company was a tither. Wallace Johnson, the founder of Holiday Inn, was a tither. John D. Rockefeller, Sr., was a tither. J.C. Penney was a tither. Are you? If not, let me challenge you to accept God's challenge and start tithing this week and continue tithing every week for the rest of your life. When you do, you're going to discover that God is a faithful God and He will literally "open the floodgates of Heaven and pour out so much blessing that you don't have room enough for it."

A FOUNDATION YOU CAN BUILD ON

Once we've established tithing as the foundation of our lives and our churches, the possibilities for ministry are limitless. Following are some recommendations of what we should do next.

1. Get out of debt.

a. Personally. Dave Ramsay says, "If you are weighed down with debt, you will have awful difficulty moving forward no matter how strong your vision is. You must get completely out of debt as soon as possible to avoid wasting your most creative time and energies on digging yourself out of a self-imposed pit."[3]

b. Corporately (your church). Jeff Berg and Jim Burgess, in their excellent book, *The Debt-Free Church,* wrote, "Virtually every debt-free ministry we have spoken to in the last several years has been delighted to be debt-free. Pastors, elders, deacons, administrators, and folks in the pews get excited when they are involved in a healthy, well-balanced ministry that is debt-free. The pastor of one of America's largest debt-free churches told us, 'Our people are so thrilled with what we see happening as a result of being out of debt [that] we will never go back to borrowing.' We discovered infectious enthusiasm and creativity in debt-free ministries."[4]

2. Stay out of debt.

Christian financial expert Larry Burkett says, "90% of all church building programs include indebtedness."[5] There's a better way to do it. Several years ago we decided not only did we want to get out of debt as a church, but we wanted to stay out. That meant we would build all future facilities, fund future programs, without long-term debt. Is it possible for a church to do that? Yes. There are a growing number of churches who are doing everything in their ministries without borrowing a dime.

We made the decision to reduce our expenditures in our annual operating budget to the level we were at six years previous in order to dedicate a significant sum of our weekly offerings to paying off our debt and preparing for future expansion. (This is how we got out of debt so fast.) We began with approximately $7,000 a week our first year. We moved it to $10,000 a week the next year. Until we got to the place where this year we have $25,000 a week set aside for nothing but future expansion. That's $1.3 million a year for nothing but future expansion and it comes out of our regular, weekly general fund offering. We don't have special offerings. All we ask our people to do is tithe each week and give an offering above the tithe as they are led by God to do so.

Here's how it's worked for us. In 1995 we moved into our new Family Life Center that cost us $1.2 million dollars. We did a capital stewardship campaign with all the bells and whistles. We asked our people to make additional commitments over a three-year period. We printed sharp, four-color brochures. We had a big commitment banquet. We did it all. It took us seven years to raise the funds we needed to pay off our loan, with interest ("Somebody Else" was getting that money, not us!). Seven years!

We decided there had to be a better way to do it. We made adjustments in our budget and in our spending so that this year, 2001, because of what we have built into our budget for future expansion, we will be able to raise $1.3 million dollars IN ONE YEAR. Without a capital stewardship campaign, without four-color brochures, without a banquet, without asking our people for additional commitments, and here's the best part: we will be able to fund the equivalent of our Family Life Center every year until Jesus comes. What took us seven years to do before, with debt, will now take us one year without debt.

And we're not stopping there. Our goal is to get to the place where $100,000 a week is designated from our general fund offerings for future expansion. That's $5.2 million dollars a year. Think of the possibilities! What could you do for ministry, for missions, with an additional $5.2 million a year? And that's completely above and beyond all of our operating expenses. Sound impossible? It's not. We're already doing it and are well on our way to our goals. You can do it, too. It just takes determination, discipline, and dedication to stick with it.

Depending on the size of your church, you may want to start with $500 a week being designated for debt retirement and future expansion. (That's $26,000 a year.) Or if you can do $1,000 a week, it's $52,000 a year. If you can do $10,000 a week, that's over half a million dollars a year! Start with whatever you can, but stretch as far as you possibly can so you can begin reaping the benefits in your ministry. Then each year simply add to the amount you are designating until your debt is completely eliminated. Once you are debt free, start putting the money on deposit with a financial institution that will pay you interest. (That's right, "SOMEBODY ELSE" will be giving you money to add to the money you have on deposit. What a concept!)

Here's more good news. Did you know it's Biblical for us to do ministry that way? Listen to the words of Moses in Deuteronomy 28:12, "The LORD will open the heavens, the storehouse of his bounty, to send rain on your land in season and to bless all the work of your hands. You will lend to many nations but will borrow from none."

A FUTURE YOU CAN COUNT ON

What's ahead for you personally and for the church of the Lord Jesus Christ? As Christians and churches begin to apply God's simple principles for financial success, I believe we are on the verge of seeing the most phenomenal accomplishments in the history of Christianity. The possibilities for ministry and missions are almost beyond comprehension. Things we never before thought an entire denomination might accomplish in a lifetime are now being accomplished by a single local church on a regular basis. We are already seeing a vast movement among the people of God to get out of debt personally and corporately in our churches, and it is opening doors that were mere dreams up until now.

There's another growing movement in the body of Christ that is one of the most remarkable developments we've seen in evangelical Christianity. It's the growing number of huge philanthropic donations being made to churches and ministries here in America.

In 1998 Helen Gantz, age 91, died and left $1 million dollars to her church in rural Indiana. In 1998 Elaine Gabbert, who had lost her mother and husband to death, gave $1.1 million to a Baptist Children's home in east Dallas. In December of 1998 Joan Kroc, wife of the founder of McDonald's, Ray Kroc, gave $80 million to the Salvation Army. It was the largest donation in the ministry's 133-year history.

In February of 1999 a 101-year-old man named Christian Thomsen gave $1.1 million to Faith Baptist Bible College and a substantial sum to his local church through his will. In 2000 America Online chairman Steve Case and his wife Jean gave $8.35 million to the Coral Ridge Presbyterian Church and Dr. D. James Kennedy to help them with their Christian school. Last year Warren Bailey left $60 million to his local church in St. Mary's, Georgia.

The historic First Baptist Church of Dallas, where for many years the beloved W.A. Criswell served as pastor, has entire buildings that were donated by families who were members of their church. The great Prestonwood Baptist Church in Plano, Texas, began to experience phenomenal growth a number of years ago when Mary Kay Ash (Mary Kay Cosmetics) donated a huge sum for them to build a new building at a crucial time in their history.

In May of 2001 Dr. Tim LaHaye and his wife Beverly gave a dramatic $4.5 million dollar donation to Dr. Jerry Falwell and Liberty University in Lynchburg, Virginia. Dr. LaHaye is a renowned pastor, theologian, and author. Another donor who requested anonymity gave another $4.5 million dollar donation bringing the total to $9 million.

In the days ahead I believe we are getting ready to witness even more phenomenal gifts given to churches and ministries all over the world. God has given the resources to us so there will always be more than enough to reach the world with the gospel. It's just a matter of our listening to His voice and obeying His Word.

People all over the world are realizing God has blessed them to amass significant fortunes not just for the sake of accumulating vast sums of wealth, but rather to help fund His kingdom work on the earth before Jesus returns. Let me challenge you to evaluate where you are today and what God has blessed you with and ask you to consider being one of those Christian philanthropists who blesses the socks off a church or a ministry somewhere in the world. I challenge you to help your local church first, and then ask your pastor for ideas of other ministries you can help.

If we enthusiastically and consistently apply God's simple principles for financial success to our lives and to our churches, the day will come when we can all do it.

Just remember the A, B, C's!

. . . from the G.O.O.D. file

(simple ideas to encourage you to Get Out Of Debt)

The Priority of Saving

Contrary to what many Christians have been led to believe, saving money is both Biblical and practical. Solomon wrote in Proverbs 13:11, "Dishonest money dwindles away, but he who gathers money little by little makes it grow."

Saving money is both Biblical and practical. And the discipline of saving something from each paycheck will provide benefits and blessings you will be grateful for the rest of your life.

Ironically it's rarely the theological ramifications that hold people back from saving. Rather it's just plain old procrastination. We plan on getting started—just not today.

Years ago I heard the following slogan: "If not now, when? If not here, where? If not you, who?" Those are good questions to ask when it comes to saving.

➤ "If not now, when do you plan on saving?" (There's no better time than right now.)

➤ "If not here, in your present job and in your present location, where will you begin?"

➤ "If not you, who's going to do it for you?" (Answer? No one.)

Even if you can only start with $5 or $10 a week, you ought to start saving today. Your ultimate goal should be the 10-10-80 plan (i.e., 10% to God, 10% to savings, and 80% to live on).

Consistent, regular savings each week over a long period of time is one of the smartest ways you can stop working for money and have your money work for you. But don't take my word for it, take Solomon's, who said that "he who gathers money little by little makes it grow."

That's G.O.O.D. advice . . . for all of us.

Action Plans

A. Make the commitment to yourself, your family, and your God that you will start saving. Begin with your next paycheck.

B. To motivate you as you save, set some goals. Dream a little and decide some short and long term goals for your savings.

C. Rejoice in the Lord as you are able to meet these goals.

ENDNOTES

Chapter One

1. *Fort Worth Star Telegram*, 25 December 1999. Copyright 1999, *Fort Worth Star Telegram*.
2. Brochure from Christian Financial Concepts, 1999. Used by permission.
3. Larry Burkett, *Debt-Free Living* (Chicago: Moody, 1989), p. 58.

Chapter Two

1. Paul and Veva Young, January, 2000. Used by permission.
2. Mark and Vera Strickland, January, 2000. Used by permission.
3. C. Peter Wagner, *Churchquake* (Ventura, CA: Regal Books, 1999), pp. 243-244.
4. Ibid.
5. Ibid.
6. Ibid.
7. Larry Burkett, *Debt-Free Living*, p. 57.
8. Mary Hunt, *Debt-Proof Living* (Nashville: Broadman & Holman, 1999), pp. 65-66.
9. Ibid., p. 11.

Chapter Three

1. John Hagee, from the tape, "Twelve Principles of Prosperity," John Hagee Ministries, 1999. Used by permission.

Chapter Four

1. Article in *Fort Worth Star Telegram*, 16 January 2000. Copyright 2000, *Fort Worth Star Telegram*.
2. Larry Burkett, "Questions and Answers," Web site article, Christian Financial Concepts, January 18, 2000. Used by permission.

Chapter Five

1. Larry Burkett, *Answers to Your Family's Financial Questions* (Pomona, CA: Focus on the Family, 1987), pp. 106-107.
2. Gary Moore, *Ten Golden Rules for Financial Success* (Grand Rapids: Zondervan, 1996), pp. 141-142.

Chapter Six

1. Larry Burkett, *Christian Financial Concepts Newsletter*, January, 2001. Used by permission.
2. Dr. Homer G. Lindsay, former pastor of First Baptist Church in Jacksonville, Florida. Used by permission.
3. Dave Ramsay, *How to Have More Than Enough* (New York: Penguin, 2000), p. 78.
4. Jeff Berg and Jim Burgess, *The Debt-Free Church* (Chicago: Moody, 1996), pp. 15-16.
5. Ibid., p. 119.

Appendix A

Sample Budget
for Getting Out of Debt

The next five pages present a simple budget consisting of five elements that *anyone* can use.

1) A *financial overview* of three things:
    (1) remaining *debt*
    (2) current *savings*
    (3) unpaid *bills*

2) *Annual expenses* and obligations in detail

3) A *weekly expense* budget that guides spending

4) A *monthly expense* budget detailing obligations

5) *Retirement accounts* updating the growth of funds

Don't use the word "budget" if you don't want to. Call it your "G.O.O.D. File." It is your get-out-of-debt plan, and it will keep you on track toward your financial goals. Simply plug in *your own* numbers and totals and you're ready to go. Keep it updated weekly on your computer and also file a hard copy.

Every week print a copy of page one. If you're married, share this with your mate so you are both always aware of the obligations you have and the progress you are making. This will serve as an ongoing motivation for you to get out of debt as quickly as possible.

Getting Out of Debt
Financial Overview

A. Remaining Debt as of 12/27/02

$22,470.72	GMAC (Bob's car)
18,999.60	TMC (Carla's car)
3,815.00	Mastercard
2,756.16	Upland Motorsports
1,670.50	VISA
$49,711.98	**(Total remaining debt)**

B. Savings as of 12/27/02

$1,500.00   First Federal (Emergency Fund)
            Account #79832-293

C. Outstanding Bills as of 12/27/02

$ 557.00	Rent/Mortgage Payment (1/05/03)
468.14	Bob's car payment (1/15/03)
316.60	Carla's car payment (1/20/03)
229.68	Waverunner payment (1/22/03)
151.33	Car Insurance (1/25/03)
$1,722.75	**(Total)**

Getting Out of Debt
Annual Expenses
as of 12/27/02

Annual Income: $66,719.64 (1,283.07 per week gross)
Approximate Disposable Income: $55,780.00
    (1,072.69 per week net)
Savings Goal: $1,040.00 ($20.00 per week)

Annual Expenses:

$ 6,672.00	Tithe
1,040.00	Savings
6,684.00	Rent/House payment
$ 1,260.00	Electric
1,800.00	Gas
600.00	Water
420.00	Cable
248.50	Internet
780.00	Phone
600.00	Cell phone
300.00	Long distance phone
$ 6,500.00	Groceries
520.00	Dry cleaning
$ 200.00	Renter's/Homeowner's insurance
1,825.96	Car insurance
120.00	Waverunner insurance
1,500.00	Health insurance
$ 5,617.68	Bob's car
3,799.92	Carla's car
600.00	Car maintenance
2,756.16	Waverunner payment
2,400.00	Mastercard
1,200.00	Visa

$ 520.00	Girls' allowance
2,080.00	Carla's allowance
2,080.00	Bob's allowance
600.00	Clothes allowance
600.00	Miscellaneous/Entertainment
800.00	IRA
1,000.00	401K
$55,124.22	(Total÷52=1,060.08 per week)

Getting Out of Debt
Monthly Expenses
as of 12/27/02

A. Weekly Income: $1,283.07

$ 173.07	Child support
700.00	Bob's salary
410.00	Carla's salary
$1,283.07	**(Total)**

B. Fixed Weekly Expenses:

$128.30	Tithe
20.00	Savings
40.00	Bob's allowance
40.00	Carla's allowance
125.00	Groceries
10.00	Girls' allowance
10.00	Dry cleaning
$373.30	**(Total)**

C. Amount left for other weekly expenses and obligations:

$909.77 (gross)
$699.39 (net)

Getting Out of Debt
Weekly Expenses

A. Monthly Expense Budget:

$55,124.22 divided by 12=$4,593.68
(Please see "Annual Budget" on pages 127–128)

B. Monthly Credit Card/Loan Payments:

$229.68	Waverunner
200.00	Mastercard
100.00	VISA
$529.68	

C. Total Monthly Net Income:

Total Monthly Net Income:	$4,644.74
Total Fixed Monthly Expenses:	4,590.14
Difference	$ 54.60

Getting Out of Debt
Retirement Funds
as of 12/27/02

Morgan Stanley $31,150.88—IRAs
                               (Account #290342-392
                               and #290342-393)

401K (GM) $28,140.34
                               (Account #189204)

Total Retirement: **$59,291.22**

Appendix B

The ACC Weekly—a free, e-mail newsletter
by Barry L. Cameron

SPIRITUAL SHOPLIFTERS

According to a recent study done by the University of Florida, shoplifting has reached epidemic proportions in America. This rather innocuous and allegedly victimless crime takes place every ten seconds somewhere in our country. And those are only the cases stores have reported.

The total retail losses will amount to more than $25 billion dollars this year, and contrary to the popular notion, there are real, live victims here. You want to venture a guess as to who those real victims are? YOU and I!

The vast majority of stores already increase their prices to help offset those who sneak in, steal something, and walk out with a smile on their face and something in their pocket. And you and I are left holding the bag. Or should I say the bill?

Admittedly it's hard to find someone who hasn't taken something that wasn't his when he was a child. Like a roll of mints, some bubble gum, a doll, or a small toy. What parent hasn't been surprised at one time or another to see something in the hands of their child after a shopping excursion and had to ask, "Where did you get that?" That's why so many people mistakenly view shoplifting as an insignificant, unimportant fact of life. After all they're just kids. And we've all done it.

But what if your teenager was coming home from shopping trips with stuff she didn't pay for? Or your husband or wife came home with bags or boxes of stuff you knew he or she didn't pay for? Would you wink at that and excuse it as something insignificant or unimportant? I don't think so. In fact, I'm pretty sure you'd know you had a major problem. A crime to be more accurate.

The fact is, the startling statistics will show the majority of shoplifters in America are not someone's little, immature kid taking a piece of bubble gum or some little matchbox toy. Rather it's grown adults who should know better. And the average theft is approximately $30! Is that unbelievable? It is to me. Is it criminal? It is to those who enforce the laws here in our country.

Unfortunately there's a far more outrageous offense being committed in America's churches that actually eclipses what's happening in America's businesses. It's the rampant rise of spiritual shoplifting. As unbelievable as it may seem to you, the statistics will show that the vast majority of people who walk into the average church in America every week give absolutely nothing. You read it right. Nothing. Zip. Zero. They don't give a thing. They've come to shoplift! Taking whatever they can get without taking on any responsibility. After all, "salvation is free," they'll say. "Shouldn't everything else be as well?" Completely ignoring the fact their salvation was anything but free. It cost God His only Son, and Jesus, His life. Someone always pays a price before anyone receives a blessing.

Now if it were someone's little immature kid doing this (spiritual shoplifting), we might be able to wink at it and excuse it by saying, "They don't know any better." But the fact is, in most cases these are individuals who've been saved (?) and members of our churches for years. Many have become so proficient at spiritual shoplifting, they're able to somehow weasel their way into leadership and teaching positions, smiling and looking sufficiently spiritual so as to deceive the masses but not the detection of the Master (Hebrews 4:13; Matthew 7:21-23).

I'm quite confident if the Lord Jesus Christ walked into the average church in America today, He'd clean the place out and say, "You've turned My Father's house into a den of thieves."

Is spiritual shoplifting a victimless crime? Not on your life. My guess is that the aggregate loss to the body of Christ far exceeds $25 billion each year. The fact there are so many unmet needs, so many churches hindered and barely hobbling in their ministries due to a lack of funds, or ministries borrowing money to do what they believe God called them to do is a telling testimony to the spiritual shoplifters among us.

God never intended the church to be like that. In fact, He intends for His church to be the best-run, best-funded institution on the face of the earth.

> The LORD will open the heavens, the storehouse of his bounty, to send rain on your land in season and to bless all the work of your hands. You will lend to many nations but will borrow from none. The LORD will make you the head, not the tail. If you pay attention to the commands of the LORD your God that I give you this day and carefully follow them, you will always be at the top, never at the bottom. Do not turn aside from any of the commands I give you today, to the right or to the left, following other gods and serving them (Deuteronomy 28:12-14).

How does He plan for us to do that? By every one of us being, at the very least, a tither of our weekly income and giving above and beyond that as He blesses us (Malachi 3:8-10; Leviticus 27:30; Matthew 22:15-22; 23:23; Luke 6:38; 1 Corinthians 16:1-2; 2 Corinthians 8:1-7; 9:1-11).

What would happen if we were able to totally eliminate spiritual shoplifting from our churches and instead educate our people to be tithers every week of their lives? What would happen if we could get every church member to give beyond the tithe as the Lord blesses and keep doing it enthusiastically and faithfully until He returns? In most cases church offerings could double or triple immediately. New ministries could begin and new staff could be hired instantly. New facilities would be built without debt. Missionaries could be placed on every foreign field in the world, fully equipped and fully supported in a matter of weeks. Bible colleges and seminaries could be fully endowed and students could train for leadership ministry for free. The list is endless.

So to all the spiritual shoplifters out there, the nontithers whose thievery is actually and quite Biblically criminal, whose actions are crippling the cause of Christ, you have two choices: #1—Grow up and stop acting like someone's immature little kid who doesn't know any better and start tithing. This week. Or #2—Go ahead and get mad. Ignore the conviction of the Holy Spirit and quit the church. In which case the church will lose absolutely nothing. Zip. Zero.

And all God's faithful tithers said?

WAIT A MINUTE!

Sunday, December 17, 2000, was one of the bloodiest days in the history of Italy. And the Mafia had nothing to do with it. It happened in the Italian Alps when a cold spell coated the mountainsides with a sheet of ice that proved deadly for a group of climbers. One after another, an Italian climber, his dog, and three others who tried to rescue them, fell some 1600 feet to their deaths.

It all began when Luigi Lazzaretti, who had been hiking with his two huskies Sasha and Zara, happened upon one of the ice-covered slopes. Sasha slipped, and instinctively, Luigi tried to catch his dog. As he did, he lost his footing and started the fatal descent down the side of the mountain, taking his other huskie, Zara with him.

Within minutes, a witness said, all you could hear were people shouting for Luigi and calling for someone to help. A man known for his expert climbing abilities was quickly summoned. Unfortunately as he attempted to help, he fell to his death. Another man tried to help as well as another after him. Tragically both of them plunged to their deaths.

"There was a chain of the dead," recounted Danilo Barbiscotti, who took part in the failed rescue effort on the 7,920-foot high Mount Arera. When the trained Alpine rescuers finally arrived to the pile of bodies at the bottom of the slope, ironically it was Sasha, the original huskie who'd slipped, who was still alive.

Now get the picture. Four men fell to an absolutely unnecessary death all because they got in a hurry and felt they needed to do something. The cold reality of the matter is that all they really needed to do was simply wait. One of the rescuers recounted, "As we were trying to get the first climber, we saw the others falling."

Honestly none of us like to wait. We don't like to wait in line. We don't like to wait for our food. We don't like to wait at the bank. We don't like to wait anywhere for anything. Period. We don't even like to wait on God.

So listen carefully. Before you get out on the slippery slopes that will most certainly lead to a calamitous conclusion: better wait a minute. You've got nothing to lose by controlling your impetuous impulses. Especially when it comes to God. Because He's always on time and always has your best interest at heart. All you need to do is wait.

"They that wait upon the LORD shall renew their strength; they shall mount up with wings as eagles; they shall run, and not be weary; and they shall walk, and not faint" (Isaiah 40:31, KJV).

BEWARE THE ELEPHANT SMUGGLERS

Officials in Mexico are still trying to figure out how they did it. Somehow someone was able to sneak "Benny" across the border at the Matamoros checkpoint. Ordinarily it wouldn't make the news. After all, smuggling of one kind or another happens almost on a daily basis between the United States and Mexico. But since "Benny" is a 9-year-old, Indian elephant who weighs 3 tons and stands 10 feet tall, Mexican authorities are steaming about it. Especially when it was discovered that "Benny" came across the border into Matamoros in a wooden box on a flatbed truck.

Guillermo Vazquez, one of the owners of the circus where "Benny" has been performing in Mexico, said he bought the elephant in Houston for $40,000.00 and sought all the proper papers for export. He became frustrated with all the red tape, bureaucracy, and delays and decided to hire a "coyote" (a professional smuggler) to sneak the elephant into Mexico.

"He's a very nice elephant," Vazquez told the *Washington Post*. "I know I made a mistake. But I did it because people want to see elephants in their circus. You know what I mean."

Now that's quite a stretch, rationalizing elephant smuggling. Wouldn't you agree? But when you think about it, probably not much more of a stretch than the rationalizations we try to give on a regular basis for the things we try to smuggle into our lives without God noticing.

Most of us don't hire "coyotes" to help us since we've had so many years of practice. Just a little compromise here, a little indulgence there, a little sin wrapped up so neatly that we think we can cross the border in broad daylight and no one will ever know, especially God.

But the truth of the matter is Numbers 32:23 says, "Be careful, your sin will find you out." Someone will blow the whistle. Someone will see. Someone will find out. Somehow. Somewhere. You'll get caught. Count on it.

We hide a lot behind the expensive suits, designer dresses, and the disarming smiles, trying to give the false impression that everything's okay when in reality we've got an elephant-sized sin we're trying to sneak by our friends, family, and fellow church members.

Take some incredibly good advice: declare what's in your life today. Confess your sin. Repent of it, renounce it, and receive forgiveness for it. Because if you don't, there's a border Guard up ahead Who's going to expose it all, and then you're really going to be in trouble.

"Nothing in all creation is hidden from God's sight. Everything is uncovered and laid bare before the eyes of him to whom we must give account" (Hebrews 4:13).

WHAT'S THE POINT?

A scandal had been brewing in Norway over the August 25, 2001, wedding of Crown Prince Haakon and his bride Mette-Marit Tjessem Hoiby. No, it's not her name that had many Norwegians in a royal huff. It's not even the fact she was an unwed mother with a 4-year-old boy. More than half of the country's first-born children have been born to unwed mothers.

It's not the fact she was a former waitress or that she has been reported to have been involved with drugs. The father of her boy is in prison because of cocaine possession, and she had been seen at numerous parties where illegal drugs were used. It's not even the fact that Crown Prince Haakon and his bride had been living together for six months prior to the wedding. Cohabitation is routinely accepted in Norway.

So what's the big scandal? Simply this. A growing number of Norwegians are wondering out loud: "If the royal family is like everyone else, who needs them?" Political scientist Bernt Aardal said, "Being part of the royal family is not like being part of other families. You can't be above the people and be one of the people at the same time."

The scandal had widened thanks to the Crown Prince's sister Martha, who was photographed in the company of Ari Behn, a young writer involved in questionable activities. They were both seen on Norwegian TV in the company of prostitutes, some of whom were sniffing cocaine. Behn insisted he was merely reporting on their Las Vegas lifestyle and not endorsing it or engaging in it. Still the reaction was one of outrage.

"This is just getting worse and worse," said Deputy Minister of Municipalities Einar Gelius in Norway's largest newspaper *Verdens Gang*. "First Mette-Marit Tjessem Hoiby's unrestrained partying, and now Ari Behn wading in women and dope. The monarchy is digging its own grave."

There's another royal family presently endangering their standing not only among the people of Norway but people all over the world. And this scandal is much worse and will have far greater ramifications than the Crown Prince and his bride ever imagined. This royal family is the church.

In speaking of the church the Bible says, "But you are a chosen people, a royal priesthood, a holy nation, a people belonging to God" (1 Peter 2:9). The King James Version says the church is to be a "peculiar" people. Sadly, in far too many cases the only thing peculiar about us is that we are so much like the world.

Peter went on to say, "Dear friends, I urge you, as aliens and strangers in the world, to abstain from sinful desires, which war against your soul. Live such good lives among the pagans that, though they accuse you of doing wrong, they may see your good deeds and glorify God on the day he visits us" (1 Peter 2:11-12).

If we don't, the world will look at us and say, "What's the point? Who needs them?"

HAS THE CONTEMPORARY CHURCH BECOME A NON-PROPHET ORGANIZATION?

I was in Los Angeles when I heard the news, and I'll never forget it. It was Thursday night, March 29th, 2001. A chartered jet crashed into a hillside just a few hundred yards short of the runway in Aspen, Colorado. Evidently the Gulfstream III twin turbojet reached the resort about 7 p.m. The Aspen airport is about 7800 feet up in the Rocky Mountains.

The chartered plane with 15 passengers and three crew members on board had already abandoned its initial approach and circled around in the heavy snowfall for a second attempt at landing. According to the Los Angeles Times, "Two other chartered jets—one immediately ahead of the doomed plane and one behind—also missed their first passes at the landing strip, pulling up at the last moment, several sources said. Neither risked a second try, rerouting instead to another airport as poor weather and darkness closed in."

It was reported that just after 7 p.m., the pilot had asked the tower if the runway lights were on. The tower said yes and asked if they were in sight. Six seconds later the pilot answered yes. That would be his last transmission. Moments later the plane slammed into the hillside wing first.

What makes this accident even more tragic is the fact that two days before the crash the Federal Aviation Administration had issued a warning that planes should not be allowed to make instrument landings at the Aspen airport at night. But apparently they never got it.

The flight had originated from Burbank with a brief stop in Los Angeles. According to Carol Carmody, the National Transportation Safety Board's acting chairwoman, during that brief stop the pilot had received the warning, but it was not written clearly and the pilot may not have understood it.

Consequently 18 people died completely unnecessarily. All because they didn't get the warning that could've saved their lives.

As you consider the contemporary evangelical scene, one can't help but wonder if there isn't an even greater tragedy looming on the horizon. This time the concern is not with pilots but rather with pulpits where the very warnings that could save people's lives are rarely being heard anymore.

The apostle Paul, who said, "Remember that for three years I never stopped warning each of you night and day with tears" (Acts 20:31), would be woefully out of place and awkwardly out of step in many contemporary churches where the wooing of seekers has replaced the warning of sinners.

John the Baptist, whose casual dress (to be quite honest) would fit right in with a majority of contemporary churches, would get kicked out for his convicting denunciations against sin. Using terms like "brood of vipers" and preaching about repentance won't get you many speaking engagements. In fact, it was John's preaching, especially his strong stand against the sins of the political leaders of his day, that got him beheaded.

Jonathan Edwards' famous sermon, "Sinners in the Hands of an Angry God," or R.G. Lee's "Payday Someday" wouldn't attract a very big crowd to the coffee cafe in most modern church atriums but those sermons did bring crowds of people to the altar. And their lives were saved because of it.

Paul's encouragement to Timothy, his young son in the faith, was, "In the presence of God and of Christ Jesus, who will judge the living and the dead, and in view of his appearing and his kingdom, I give you this charge: Preach the Word; be prepared in season and out of season; correct, rebuke and encourage—with great patience and careful instruction. For the time will come when men will not put up with sound doctrine" (2 Timothy 4:1-3a).

Strangely and quite unnecessarily, more often than not we may be doing more harm than good. On that Gulfstream III twin turbojet back in March people were provided a wonderful, enjoyable ride, first-class accommodations, and the promise of a safe landing, only to have their destinies abruptly and irreversibly changed forever because they didn't get the warning they needed most.

Shouldn't we do everything we possibly can to avoid another senseless and totally unnecessary tragedy? Absolutely! But how? Simple. Preach the Word! (2 Timothy 4:1-5). Don't hold back or hesitate to proclaim the whole counsel of God! (Acts 20:27). And, finally, be a "watchman" and sound the warnings God has given in His Word (Ezekiel 33:1-9).

If we don't . . . their blood will be on *our* hands.

RECOMMENDED READING

Akin, H.L. Bert. *The Pastor's Complete Guide to Personal Financial Planning*. Nashville: Nelson, 1993.

Barnett, Joe R. *The People Who Tested God*. Austin: Sweet Publishing, 1979.

Berg, Jeff, and Jim Burgess. *The Debt-Free Church*. Chicago: Moody, 1996.

Blue, Ron. *Generous Living*. Grand Rapids: Zondervan, 1997.

_____. *Master Your Money*. Nashville: Lifeway, 1990.

_____. *Money Talks, So Can We*. Grand Rapids: Zondervan, 1999.

Burkett, Larry. *The Complete Financial Guide for Young Couples*. Wheaton, IL: Victor, 1989.

_____. *The Complete Guide to Managing Your Money*. New York: Inspirational Press, 1996.

_____. *Debt Free Investing*. Chicago: Moody, 1995.

_____. *Debt-Free Living*. Chicago: Moody, 1989.

_____. *Dollars and $ense*. Uhrichsville, OH: Barbour, 1997.

_____. *The Financial Guide for the Single Parent*. Chicago: Moody, 1997.

_____. *Financial Parenting*. Colorado Springs: Chariot Victor, 1996.

_____. *Money before Marriage*. Chicago: Moody, 1996.

_____. *Money in Marriage*. Chicago: Moody, 1999.

_____. *Investing for the Future*. Wheaton, IL: Victor, 1992.

_____. *Preparing for Retirement*. Chicago: Moody, 1992.

_____. *Using Your Money Wisely*. Chicago: Moody, 1985.

_____. *Women Leaving the Workplace*. Chicago: Moody, 1995.

_____. *The Word on Finances*. Chicago: Moody, 1994.

_____. *Your Child and Money*. Chicago: Moody, 2000.

_____. *Your Complete Guide to Financial Security*. New York: Inspirational Press, 1992.

Dollar, Truman. *How to Carry Out God's Stewardship Plan*. Nashville: Nelson, 1974.

Eisenson, Marc. *The Banker's Secret*. New York: Villard, 1984.

Howard, Alton. *Money Grows on Trees*. West Monroe, LA: Howard, 1994.

Hunt, Mary. *Debt-Proof Living*. Nashville: Broadman/Holman, 1999.

_____. *Debt-Proof Your Kids*. Nashville: Broadman/Holman, 1998.

Jeavons, Thomas H., and Rebekah Burch Basinger. *Growing Givers' Hearts*. San Francisco: Jossey-Bass, 2000.

Kiyosaki, Robert T. *The Cashflow Quadrant*. New York: Warner Books, 1998.

_____. *Rich Dad, Poor Dad*. New York: Warner Books, 1997.

_____. *Rich Kid, Smart Kid*. New York: Warner Books, 2000.

Lloyd, Nancy. *Simple Money Solutions*. New York: Random House, 2000.

MacArthur, John. *Whose Money Is It, Anyway?* Nashville: Word, 2000.

Miller, Peter G. *The Common Sense Mortgage*. New York: Harper & Row, 1987.

Olford, Stephen. *The Grace of Giving*. Grand Rapids: Kregel, 2000.

Orman, Suze. *The Courage to Be Rich*. New York: Riverhead, 1999.

_____. *The 9 Steps to Financial Freedom*. New York: Crown, 1997.

Paris, James L. *Financial Boot Camp*. Lake Mary, FL: Creation House, 1992.

Pollan, Stephen M., and Mark Levine. *Live Rich*. New York: Harper Business, 1998.

Ramsay, Dave. *Financial Peace*. New York: Viking, 1997.

_____. *How to Have More Than Enough*. New York: Penguin, 2000.

_____. *More Than Enough*. New York: Viking, 1997.

Russell, Bob. *Money: A User's Manual*. Sisters, OR: Multnomah, 1997.

Stanley, Thomas. *The Millionaire Mind*. Kansas City, MO: Andrews McMeel, 2000.

_____. *The Millionaire Next Door*. Marietta, GA: Longstreet Press, 1996.

Taylor, Jack R. *God's Miraculous Plan of Economy*. Nashville: Broadman, 1975.

Temple, Todd. *Money: How to Make It, Spend It and Keep Lots of It*. Nashville: Broadman/Holman, 1998.

Watts, Wayne. *The Gift of Giving*. Colorado Springs: NavPress, 1982.

The Newcomer's Guide to the Bible:
Themes and Timelines
Michael C. Armour

Here is the tool you have been looking for, to introduce new believers to the Word of God. This resource has been designed and written in a way that helps people who have had little or no exposure to the Word of God to quickly gain a basic understanding of the Bible. This is a great starting point for further study of God's Word that will be fruitful and life changing. This resource can also be used as a refresher course for people who have long been familiar with the Bible. Every church should have this book available in its library.

300 pages, soft, ABC01-859-3 $14.99

COLLEGE PRESS PUBLISHING COMPANY
1.800.289.3300 • www.collegepress.com

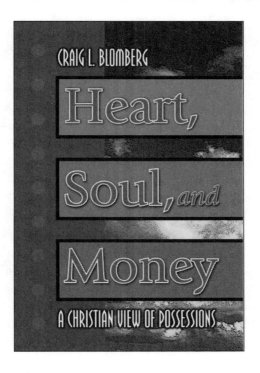

Heart, Soul, and Money:
A Christian's View of Possessions
Craig Blomberg

As more and more Christians become wealthier than any generation before them, giving has steadily decreased. For many
Christians this disparity is not due to willful disobedience, but to
a lack of knowledge of the biblical teaching regarding the Christian's
responsibility to give. This challenging study will help you and your
group to gain a biblical perspective of wealth. Your members will be
blessed as they come to realize the wonderful results that come with
generous, faithful giving. Your local congregation, other ministries, and
people in need will be blessed as God works through the increased giving that is sure to result from this study.

90 pages, soft, ABC01-844-5 $8.99

 COLLEGE PRESS PUBLISHING COMPANY
1.800.289.3300 • www.collegepress.com